LEAD ME
to the
EXIT

by
ELLEN C. MOORE

Ariadne Press
Washington, D.C.

Library of Congress Cataloging in Publication Data

Moore, Ellen, 1915 -
   Lead me to the exit.

Autobiography.
   1. Moore, Ellen, 1915 -   2. United States—Biography.   I. Title.
CT275.M5894A34   973.9'092'4 [B]   77-9949 ISBN O-918056-01-2

Published by Ariadne Press
4400 P Street, N.W., Washington, D.C.

To
Meredith and Connie

LEAD ME TO THE EXIT

1

There is always trouble brewing somewhere in Washington, D.C. Along with whatever our public servants were hatching along Pennsylvania in the beginning of 1971, there was also a kettle of uneasiness simmering under one of the quaint turrets of a row house a mile east of the Capitol. It was not the kind of exquisitely done up dwelling that the Restoration Association wanted to include in its spring tour, but for a certain WHOUF (White Heavy-weight Old Unitarian Female) that house represented success. Along with its huge mortgage, the place boasted three and a half bathrooms. Even one modest indoor facility was a symbol of splendor during the first third of my life, when I was an awkward, penniless kid in Ohio rushing down the back path with Jane Eyre under my ragged sweater, hoping for a quiet half-hour in seclusion if the yellowjackets weren't swarming under the seat.

I had achieved comparative luxury after thirty years of full time, low-paid employment. My master's degree in sociology had finally paid off with short hours, long vacations and a sizeable pay check. I had to remember this, since I was already fifty-six and was still paying off the loan for graduate school, and my dream of bringing new light and hope to two thousand elementary school children and their harried teachers was already beginning to fade. For every reluctant Louise whom I'd guided to the conviction that teachers were really friendly folks who would be able to give her the power to read, there were ten rebellious Roberts and runaway Rosies escaping through the broken windows. Of course I loved my job, especially the part about going home in the afternoons, but I didn't seem to have that magic touch after all, and I knew I was failing too many little Americans who had already opted to retire from the struggle to get ahead.

Not that home life was so delightful that it made up for the deficiencies I felt on the job. City life gobbles up any size income, and our house was some kind of turkey. We'd been told it was seventy-five years old and that its former inhabitants had been an energetic family of seventeen, but we'd been a little naive about the costs of remodelling. My daughters and I beat such a path to the lumber yard that we wore out the weeds. The workmen always needed another length of pipe or sheet of plywood. Although it was real satisfaction to create comfort and attractiveness throughout the house, including the new basement apartment, we often considered burning down the whole shoot-match when the bills came in. We had car troubles too. My old Valiant had been so wobbly after a buck deer in Virginia tried to run it off the road, that I knew it would flunk its safety exam before it ever got its front wheels off the concrete of the inspection lane, and there was no money to fix it.

Money wasn't the only problem. The girls and I had been happy to live in Washington where so much was going on, and with a house big enough for parties, we had bodacious mixtures of neighborhood children, poverty fighters, subway engineers and computer analysts, refugees from religious orders, and a generous sprinkling of students from Africa and Asia. Still, I had noticed that there was a hollow ring to the laughter at times, possibly dating from the last inauguration, but it was evident too during the last Christmas dinner we'd had for some thirty loners from my singles club. When one sees one's own daughters getting older and more caught up in career centered aloneness, there can be noticeable gaps in the merriment. The girls didn't pine for male company, bringing home all sorts of interesting men to meet their nutty mother, but none of them seemed determined to offer emotional security. I thought I had made a fairly good adjustment in finding zest for life in the never ending personality parade as an unattached observer, but I wanted something a little better for my daughters.

Obviously a change was due in my life, and that fact became clearer when a burglar kicked his way through our front window. Spending a hundred hard-earned dollars for window bars and new locks to make oneself a wardress for one's own prison can be pretty depressing.

Actually the change had begun two years earlier, but I hadn't caught the significance. A man I loved talked to me about the camping sub-culture and asked if I'd ever roughed it in the North Carolina mountains.

"You're out of your mind, Jeff." I think that was the way I tried to set him straight. "I'm no camper. I hate mosquitos and snakes. My knees hurt so much it would take a derrick to get me up if I sat on the ground, and I've spent too much effort getting a good bed. At my age, I'm not going to sleep on an air mattress."

He didn't believe a word I said. "I just know you're the kind of person who would love camping."

If the dearest man in the world saw me enhanced by the gleams of a fantasy camp-fire, I had to give some consideration to the idea. One April morning I borrowed a pup tent from one of my daughter Meredith's men, and a hatchet from our roomer, and sneaked off to a corner of Anacostia Park to see if I could pitch a tent. It was obvious in ten minutes that I had no such skill at all. The turf changed into concrete at my feet, the tent took off like a filled sail into the middle of a baseball game, and the hatchet twisted out of my hands and deliberately slashed my ankle.

Nuts to Jeff and his crazy ideas! Retrieving my truant tent from the midst of the snickery sandlotters, I limped home again, but that same afternoon when the sun came out and the wind died down, I piled the car with provisions, strapped the mattress from a rollaway bed on top of the car and told my daughter I was going to try a night in the open.

Meredith insisted on knowing where I was bound. "If you never show up again, I have to tell the police where to start looking."

Too green then even to know that there was a well set up campgroup within fifteen miles, I could only suggest that I would head toward Maine. Before I left, Meredith had her sister Connie on the phone to reason with me.

"Are you having some kind of identity crisis?" She inquired kindly. "Trying to find your little self, perhaps? Listen, you and I were always the sensible ones who liked being inside houses at night, remember? Even Meredith only went for that kind of stuff in her youth."

I went anyway, driving dreamily for hours on Maryland by-roads, trying to find a sunny spot out in a field where there was no tall grass for snakes and other varmints to hide in, but all such areas seemed to be inside somebody's pasture fence. It was nearly ten o'clock before I forced myself to knock on some farmer's door and ask permission to make use of his side yard. He was tolerantly amused at my explanation that I was trying to see if I had the guts to go through with such a dangerous experiment. He invited me to help myself to any location in back, where I would be out of sight of passing cars. Too late then for any attempt at orthodox camping, I just threw the tent on the ground and laid the mattress on top of it. I took off my shoes and belt, stuck the flashlight under my pillow and wrapped myself in a blanket. That was how I got one of the more outstanding surprises of my ever surprising life. I liked being outdoors.!

The stars were so sharply bright in a deep indigo blue sky that I didn't want to sleep at all. Except for a whippoorwill calling from the woods and jet passengers blinking their way across my soaring roof, I was all alone, and not a bit afraid. Only once when I thought I saw a dark shape slithering in the grass beside me did I reach for the flashlight in panic, but it was only my belt, as harmless and innocent as the stars.

At morning I washed my face by wiping off the cool dew that covered my cheeks, and built a twig fire between flat stones so that I could boil eggs in a tin can and make coffee. It was my first outdoor breakfast, and the knowledge that I had to go back to the dirty, crowded, glass-strewn city made it taste especially good. Once again my prediction about what the future held for me had been all wrong. How exhilarating it is to know that one can be completely mistaken.

That's been the story of my life. All along, one disillusionment followed another, and many times the reality has been far better than the expectation. But even with that night of wonder to bolster faith, I still saw the future as dreary in 1971.

I expected to be stuck forever in a job that would have ever dwindling satisfactions. I couldn't quit because I was at the age when jobs of any kind are hard to get. I didn't really want a job at all. What I dreamed about was taking off across the country like a vagabond, giving up my hard-won, established life, but I knew I could never do that. My late husband had not been a big earner. If I did arrive at social security age, I wouldn't get enough to live on, and most of my long years of work had not been covered with retirement planning. If I continued with the school board until I was seventy-one, I might get some such amount as twenty-five dollars a month, since my tenure had been so short, and that hardly seemed worth while.

Still, the notion to take off was strong, and one wintry day, on a completely mad impulse, I made a down payment on an old camper van that I found huddled against the back fence in some used car lot in Clinton, Maryland. I might not get much use out of it, since no sensible person quits a job unless something better comes up, and I didn't even have a place to park the van, but I had to have it.

A six month's bout with asthmatic bronchitis threatened to finish me off, but in the end actually saved me. I caught the cold that started it all by camping in a dank Virginia woods in January, and I coughed all through February. In March I began hauling home filled prescriptions by the bucketful, and none of them did any good. When my breath gave out, the doctor told me casually by phone that I was beginning emphysema and should see a specialist. On my way to keep that appointment, I stopped at the library to read up about my ailment and came across the statement that "death sometimes occurs within a few years of the first shortness of breath."

Since I had never smoked in my life, having my air shut off for the last few years of life seemed grossly unfair, and it pushed me over the edge. The specialist changed all the medication, advised me to buy a machine to help me breathe, and said I had a good chance of recovery.

Suspecting that he said the same thing to all terminal patients, I craftily began making my escape by asking him if he would recommend an extended leave of absence, and he said he'd go along with that.

At home I talked it over with Meredith, and she sadly agreed that if I wanted to go off somewhere and make free use of whatever time I had left, we'd better put up the house for sale and start getting rid of possessions. In the end, there didn't seem to be time to sell the house, but the bank agreed to a refinancing loan on the strength of Meredith's potential for earning. That gave her lower monthly payments that she could manage by herself, and netted me a few hundred for the trip. It probably wouldn't be a long trip anyway, I thought, as I labored breathlessly up and down the stairs with loads of supplies I would need for a variety of seasons and climates. My typewriter and books and painting supplies had to be tucked in somewhere. A friend gave me a mace gun and a fire extinguisher for dire emergencies, and neighbors bought whatever we had to sell, including my one evening dress, since I would never need such garb again as a camper. Meredith found renters for our little downstairs apartment as well as for the house itself, moving into another small apartment until we could see how things went.

My colleagues at work were alternately horror-struck and thrilled at what I planned to do.

"But don't you think you need to be settled somewhere if you're going to—.?" My friend left that grim question unfinished and I didn't try to answer.

"You need security now more than ever before." Another anxious friend pleaded that way.

I was no longer buying that idea. "Security for what? Anyway, are you so sure there is such an animal?"

As school ended, they took me out to lunch and had a kind of going away shower. One woman said goodbye with bright eyes. "This is the most exciting thing that ever happened to me, and it isn't even happening to me."

On the last day of school, after I had turned my final pay into traveller's checks, Connie urged me to get on my way before I had to fight the rush hour traffic. She'd come over to finish the packing for storage and clean up the house. I felt that I was deserting her when I made my last journey down the front steps with ice for the camper cooler, but a pilgrim must be willing to take advantage of those who are glad to speed the farewells, and it seemed that I was representing all those who yearned for freedom and adventure. A delegation of neighbors waved me off, everyone saying they would love to go along, except for the fact that they had payments to make on the new couch or they had to look after the grand-daughter's twins while she worked, or they couldn't leave their homes unattended because someone might break in. The most frequent unsolicited apology was made by women who might be getting a call from Charlie or Joe or Phil and couldn't bear to be away from the phone. All over the country, women have chained themselves to telephones. Even my old friend Jinny, who actually sold out in Florida saying she would join me in Ohio and go along, changed her mind at the end because she had met a new Charlie and he just might be calling one of these days.

It was just as well. The camper wasn't really big enough for more than one live person and all the dreams I was hauling for others. I was a prospector for treasure, financed by the love and good will of others who wanted to see strange new lands but had to stay at home.

Of course I didn't die, and I no longer have any time for thoughts about such nonsense, but I've had five years since that day of departure in which to gain wisdom. The cobwebs that have interfered with a clear vision of reality were blown away by months of country air and mountain breezes. As soon as I entered the shady quiet of Prince William Forest, my first night out of Washington, I was breathing more easily, and I haven't hooked up to the machine for years. Once again, I was all wrong about what lay ahead. There must have been something defective with my eyes that I was never able to see the complete picture, or perhaps I always came up with crooked conclusions because I only looked with half an eye.

As a five year old I once said, "Wouldn't it be funny if the roads ran kitty-corner across the fields instead of straight?"

My vocabulary was limited. By funny I really meant strange, curious, diverting, extraordinary, whimsical.

From the superiority of their seven and nine years my brother and sister looked at me witheringly. Apparently they'd always known that although the gravelled mile in front of our house met other thoroughfares at both ends in proper right angles, that wasn't at all typical of Ohio country roads.

"They do run kitty-corner, you dummy, and every other way too. Can't you see that?"

I really must have been a dummy. Although at the time I'd never seen a mountain road cork-screwing into the sky, I had gone for a buggy ride with my father along the road that followed the lake shore, but I hadn't noticed. Probably I was too busy eating apples we'd picked up in somebody else's orchard or learning how to say "Giddyap" with the effective note of command.

At six I thought the billy goat wanted to eat me when he came toward the bunch of buttercups I'd picked after crossing the swinging bridge from school. At seven I thought it wouldn't be too much trouble to freeze to death by sitting in a snowbank when my mother was down on me, and at eight I absolutely knew that the world would come to an end because I'd lost a library book in the attic.

At fourteen, I was still protesting to my more realistic sister that maybe some dirty-minded people had babies by doing nasty things together, but nice folks were exempt from such shameful shenanigans, and their babies got started growing because they slept together in the same bed, and what I meant by sleeping was the unconscious, dead-to-the-world type of sleeping. If Adam could sleep through having a rib removed so that a wife could be produced, it wouldn't be any trouble for God to stimulate reproduction while upper-class married people got their rest.

I was still a dummy at twenty-three when I believed that one year of graduate school at the University of Chicago was all I needed to qualify as a social worker, so that society and I could sit down together and talk over the world's problems for certain solutions.

It wasn't that I couldn't learn. I stuffed my head with books and my days with experiences of one kind or another, but every time I woke to one blinding, unassailable fact, there was always another crop of stupid assumptions to work through.

Although I should have observed from the ample evidence that two unhappy people do not find eternal joy when they join their hands in wedlock, I thought the formula would perform well for me. I had one baby under the impression that I would have a perfectly behaved child, and another with the droll notion that I had it in me to be an improvement over all other mothers. And so many hundreds of times that I have lost count, I have said, "I'll never be happy again."

I said that when a blind date disappeared after meeting me in the Chicago Public Library, when a sadistic teacher Meredith had in the fourth grade kept her out of the Christmas program because her voice wasn't pretty enough, when Connie failed algebra and began skipping school. There was also the time that a beautiful baby I'd placed for adoption was proved to be grossly brain-damaged, and the time that a dear fourteen year old girl I thought I was helping to grow in self-respect set up in business behind a blanket in a gas station, admitting it to me in despair with the words, "What difference does it make anyway? I'm nothing but a slut."

I said it again when a car I'd left inadequately braked on a hill rolled into the path of another car and badly injured another woman. And again when my marriage proved to be a disaster, and the more malicious townspeople said I'd probably driven my husband to suicide. And again when a daughter's marriage went onto the rocks.

Events like that always resulted in my having to order my lungs to pump in and out to keep the vital processes going. I was always certain also that happiness was gone forever when a man I thought was meant to be my own true love changed into an uncaring clod. There was a day that I took a short walk to a sunny hillside cemetery, and set up a date for my own demise. It would be October 16, 1968. I wasn't planning to take my life, but to learn by that time some mysterious primitive secret of how to let it end spontaneously, as I had heard the natives did in certain more intuitive cultures. By that year, I would have seen ten more glorious autumns, the girls would be full grown, and I would surely have sampled everything life had to offer.

That was long before I discovered that my feet could fly across the dance floor in perfect rhythm with the best dancer in town, before I saw that the aspen gold of Arizona is just as enchanting as the scarlet of Ohio's maples. I had no way of knowing then how much fun it would be to knock out the back wall of my western rented shack and build a six-foot clothes closet with my own hands. At that time, Connie had not earned her master's degree with honors, nor had Meredith wowed the congregation of All-Souls Unitarian Church with her innovative and perceptive sermon on security. I hadn't even written my first novel or identified the black capped phainopepla who sings from the top of a cottonwood tree in the ravine out back.

Being deeply suspicious of all who set themselves up as prophets and seers, I would not have believed anyone who tried to tell me how much better life can be when one reaches sixty. I did listen eventually though, when people told me I ought to write a book.

It wasn't when my brother said I'd better write one because I had such a big mouth about the way other people put words together, because I knew that was ridicule, and it wasn't when the neighbors in Ohio marvelled that I must be seeing so many sights in the great windy city that I should be able to write a book. That was simply an expression of their wistful hope that someday they could get out of the kitchens and berry patches, I thought.

It was many years before I could appreciate that I've really had a funny life, and by funny I still mean strange, curious, diverting, extraordinary and whimsical.

Some of my experiences have been down-right humorous as well.

IN THE LAND OF MILK AND BUTTERCUPS

2

Some sad day right after a national election, if the anti-mental health faction gets its innings, they will no doubt establish a Department for Lowering Self-Esteem. They will be missing out on a natural-born leader if they fail to appoint my brother Milton as Secretary of the whole thing. He could have handled the national program with distinction when he was no more than fourteen. Our family could have used his salary too. Two things we always had in abundance were poverty and Milton's wise-cracks.

If it wasn't born in him, I don't know where Milton could have got his pretty wit, but the inventiveness of it must have been a mutation, even if he learned some of the words from those magazines Pa brought home by the buggyful. Pa had a rich booming laugh that could be heard all over Mentor Park when he was a traffic policeman there, but he was satisfied with other people's jokes. Ma was too busy getting ahead to ridicule anyone. I expect Milton could have got some sharpness from having to wear knickerbockers and long black stockings with holes when all the other boys had long pants, or because he had to write with lead pencil when the other high school students had fountain pens. Anyway, he came out with words as mean and sharp as the point of a pencil pricking a county fair balloon.

Take that steamy, sticky corn-growing June day when my mother called us in from pulling weeds and chopping kindling. "You kids have been working too hard out in that hot sun. I got forty cents left in the sugar bowl and you can have it for a couple gallons of gas so you can go swimming."

My mother's concern that her brilliant, industrious American children would work themselves into early graves usually spurred us on to a few more hours of labor, but we weren't martyrs. Whooping with joy, we pounded upstairs to dig out our bathing suits, all wool because everyone knew you'd get pneumonia otherwise. They'd been handed down from skinnier cousins too, and it was no cinch to pull them on over sweaty bodies. If Margaret and I had ever heard that there was beauty in the nudity of a growing girl, Milton had knocked that out of our heads long since. Having no bathrobes or lighter cover-ups, Marge and I used our winter coats buttoned to the wishbone. It wasn't comfortable that way, but we could stand most anything for fifteen minutes. The beach was only four miles away. We didn't know the distance would also be peppered with flat tires.

Forty cents for gas was an enormous treat, and Milton had been driving since he was eight, so he was in a surprisingly genial mood. We hit the first flat as we were going up Henry's hill. Smiling patiently, Milton pried the tire off the rim, dipped it in the ditch to find the air bubbles, and burned on a patch at the right spot. He was hand pumping air into the tire and getting a little deflated himself when I offered to help.

His brotherly appreciation was withering. "The way you go about anything, Ellen, you'd be sucking the air out instead of pushing it in. It takes someone who knows what he's doing to pump up a tire."

Two flats later, he wasn't quite so debonair. By that time my old maroon plush was soaked clear through, so I innocently took it off. Milt flew into quite a nasty rage.

"What do you think you're doing, you crazy galoot? Do you want to get us arrested for indecent exposure? Cover up, you fat ninny. I got enough trouble. If it wasn't for you two heavy-weights squashing the air out of the tires, I'd be swimming already."

Marge straightened up from wedging a rock under the rear wheel. Her face turned into a purple cabbage popping out of a wreath of fake fur that looked like soggy corn shucks. "Pull your suit down, El," she shrieked. "Your hinder's showing."

I yanked, looked down to see how far I was showing, and then shrieked because what I had believed to be a bathing suit was really what was left of a piece of cake for a horde of hungry moths. With every yank the holes were growing larger. It must have been pretty funny. Even little brother Ben who was too sweet to make fun of big sisters collapsed on the running board laughing. I crawled back into my private sauna.

None of us laughed when the fourth tire swooshed flat. There wasn't any more tire patch, and Milton was at the end of his endurance when a car load of high-school rowdies chugged to a stop beside us and lent Milt some repair material. Margaret and I cowered on the far side of the Lizzie hoping they wouldn't notice us, but we didn't escape. They pretended they didn't recognize us.

"Who are your beautiful girl friends, Pete?" (Pete was another of Milton's names. More on that later.) "What's the matter with them. Have they got the chills?"

I expect that helped convince my brother that we were in need of further disparagement. I have forgotten how he put it, but his remarks were so effective we never doubted that we were hopelessly over-weight, muddled headed, romantically deluded and too homely to succeed at anything except as models for comic valentines. When we reached the beach that hot day so long ago, we leaped over miles of shameless bodies and wore our coats until we were up to our necks in beautiful, cool blue Lake Erie and then we tossed them onto the beach where Ben spread them out to dry.

We stayed in the water until we were blue with cold and shivered delightfully all the way home.

Now to explain about the Pete business. By a curious inheritance, three of us kids were nicknamed Pete because we looked like my father, and that was a name he had acquired as a child of eight. Grandma Crawford had so many children with plain names like Dave and Ezra that by the time she got to my father she wanted something a little fancier and named him Stillman, for a town in Illinois where some of her people had lived. Pa ran away from home to live with his Uncle Ben and Aunt Linnie when he was a feisty brat, because he'd started a complaint that even the little kids who didn't have jobs ought to have breakfast cooked for them. Grandma didn't go for that. If there was a cupful of mush, a working boy needed it, and she took after Pa with a water dipper. He never lived at home again. His aunt and uncle were kind and prosperous and didn't mind taking in a hungry nephew, but Aunt Linnie couldn't abide his name. There was a Stillman theater in Cleveland at the time, and Aunt Linnie was sure Grandma hadn't had any better sense of what was proper than to name her child after a place where the devil surely dwelled. Promptly dragging her new foster child to the church, she had him solemnly baptized Peter. Pa didn't care much what he was called. Pete was fine for everyday purposes but for such things as signing on deeds or pension checks, he stuck to his legal name. A name from the Bible pleased Aunt Linnie. Three good meals a day pleased Pa.

Milton and Marge and I were like Pa in many ways. We were thick featured, red faced and very fond of filling our bellies. Ben was more delicate, and it was so hard to find something that would stay on his stomach that he had rickets as a baby, and all his hair came out by the handful. I would have welcomed a mild case of rickets if it had made me pale and slender, because I thought that looking like a Crawford branded me with a repulsive identity; so I always tried to reject what my father stood for and be on my mother's side when they had those disgraceful family arguments. They weren't really fights, though, because my father only whistled through his teeth while Ma yelled.

My mother came to the holy land of America as an orphaned fourteen year old, avid to fight for what she thought were American ideals: getting ahead in life, putting on a good show, and adopting refinements. She also held out for a little more in life than her four sisters got because they all married dour German men and had to put up with old German customs that made servants out of wives. Ma held out for an American, someone who cared for a little life and humor instead of continuous gloom and hard work. Her sister Pauline's husband said she looked through the whole woods and then picked out a crooked stick after all, but that wasn't fair. My father wasn't crooked. He just liked a little life and humor instead of continuous gloom and hard work. My mother spent the forty years of their married life trying to mold him into a model hardworking German husband.

I always thought it was a pretty chancy thing that she found him at all, thereby giving the four of us our turn at bat. She was a maid-of-all-work for a family whose elaborate house was set back from the road in Euclid, Ohio. It was pretty lonesome for a girl back there, so as she hung up the hemstitched sheets and picked the butter beans, my mother watched the road and waved to everyone who looked familiar. She couldn't quite make out the people, but she thought she recognized the rigs, and there was one team of grey horses she was sure belonged to her brother-in-law Paul. Instead, it was my young father, driving an oil wagon for a few months until the weather got warm enough for the hobo life he preferred. Intrigued by the girl who was so anxious to attract his attention, he obligingly called the house from the station a mile down the hill. The phone must have been a rarity in 1909, and I can imagine that Ma plucked it off the wall nervously and shouted hello. I've nearly always been glad that at the time they hadn't popularized that loneliness guarantee, the unlisted phone.

My father's opening words, I understand, were, "This is Mr. Turnover speaking. Do I have the honor of addressing Alice?"

"There is no Alice here," said my unsuspecting mother. "Do you mean Anna?"

"Anna, to be sure. And how is the prettiest girl on Chardon Road this lovely evening?"

My mother had been engaged for six long years to another man, and she was in a process of adjustment to hearing the banns read for him and some other girl in the

Lutheran church they all attended. She must have found flattery warm and cheering, but she gamely protested that she didn't know any Mr. Turnover.

Pa acted suitably hurt. "How could you forget our last dance together? I will never forget."

She gave him the clues right on schedule. "You mean the dance at the Collinwood Fire Department?"

"Ah, I knew you hadn't forgotten. I'll be up to see you in twenty minutes, darling. I have to go now. My horse is getting restless."

My mother was pretty sure she'd never before seen that fresh imposter when he arrived at the back door, but she couldn't very well say so when the lady of the house was standing right there giving her the menu for Sunday dinner. By the time he'd ingratiated himself to the lady by saying he'd never had the pleasure of seeing such beautiful flower beds, and owned to the Crawford name, it was too late for Ma to be indignant. Determined that she would never go through another long engagement, my mother married him in six weeks.

They stuck it out together until my father died in his seventies. He allowed himself to be tamed a bit; falling for the appeal of a "place of our own where nobody can tell us to get out." He'd had all he could stand of working for rich people by the time I was four. With a seventy-five dollar shanty which he moved by haywagon to a ten acre plot of woods, we had everything we'd ever need, Pa said. There was running water in a ditch two hundred feet away, free fuel growing all around us, lots of thistles for a pair of milk goats to mow down, room in the corners of the shanty for our beds, and a glorious never-ending supply of stumps to pull. There was only one thing my father liked better than cleaning ditches and that was pulling stumps.

My mother had other ideas about priorities. "Pa, we ain't going to live here like gypsies. You're going to build us a clothes closet or I'll know the reason why."

Pa laid down the ax he was honing and drove half a dozen spikes into the wall beside the door. "There's your clothes closet, Ma. Now get that boy out of bed to help me pull stumps."

Ma had to make do with a curtain hung around the spikes. She had other high and mighty ideas too. She wanted a basement under the house with a furnace, linoleum on the kitchen floor, a short-chimney oil stove for cooking, pretty ribbons for her daughters' hair and white shoes for their feet. In time she achieved some of her ideals, but they were never quite right. The oil stove was too short for the wash boiler and you couldn't cook anything else when the water was heating. We finally got the basement and a pipeless furnace. We even had a kitchen sink with a pump, but the water it brought up was what stood in the basement whenever the rain came down hard.

My mother cried when my father bought us white sneakers to wear to the school entertainment, and he couldn't understand why. "You said you wanted them to have white shoes."

What she'd had in mind were leather slippers that buttoned prettily across our ankles, but Pa said tennis shoes were lots cheaper. Ma went around rehearsing a little speech she could make in case anyone rudely implied that we were unsuitably shod. "Their feet are growing so fast that my husband and I don't think it pays to buy good shoe leather for them to outgrow."

In the same spirit she would invite people into the house. "Come in if you can get in. We're just camping here until we get our house built."

It was a bitter struggle for Ma to put on a good show when Pa thought the good things of life came for nothing if you weren't too fussy about how you got them. You didn't need medicine when there was dandelion and dock and wild garlic growing in the fields. He learned to drive a car, but he gave that up quite cheerfully when he became so fat and clumsy that his feet got tangled up in the pedals and he sent the little Ford coupe crashing through a gas pump. It didn't matter much that he no longer had modern transportation. Walking was good, and there was nearly always somebody going his way.

While Ma yearned over furniture in the Sears catalogue, Pa was forever standing in the right place when old things were being given away. One time my brother was girl-watching on a corner in Painesville, when he was hailed by a school buddy. "Hey, Pete, what's your old man doing sitting on the sidewalk in a swivel chair in Mentor?"

Milt guessed he better find out. Pa was waiting patiently for a ride home, which would no doubt materialize from somewhere, because it would have been a trifle awkward walking and carrying his latest donation. He had happened to be on the spot when the insurance man had some new office furniture delivered.

A weekly pay check for her husband would have been paradise to Ma. Pa was willing to work. No one ever spent more energy than he at chopping stumps, and during the winter he had no objection to a watchman job, but he always said his best friend was Uncle Sam. The best decision he ever made in his life was to sign up for the Spanish American War. He was talking economics, not patriotism, although he had always admired the flag and said he wanted to have one on his coffin since a veteran could get one free. Midway through Pa's whimsical career of supporting a family, he began to draw a ten dollar a week veteran's pension. Not sufficient for paying all the bills, it still drove off any wolf cub of worry that might have been hanging around Pa's door. He learned then to develop ailments that would gain him vacations in Veteran's Hospitals, and his dream for the last years of his life was to retire to the domiciliary at Bay Pines, Florida.

My mother would hover over him when he was planning a trip. "Pa, you can't wear that old shirt. It looks terrible. I got your suit pressed and I picked out this striped tie for you."

She never accepted the rules of the game Pa played with the Uncle of us all. When he presented himself humbly ragged at Crile or Hines, he might be issued a clothing outfit. He never enjoyed an overcoat that he paid for as much as the one the government gave him when he obviously couldn't be allowed to go home without a coat on a winter day, a man just out of a sick bed.

In our county Pa discovered that juries are picked not quite by random, so he angled to get on the pay roll of Uncle's country cousin, the Lake county government, for about two weeks a year. He proudly wore his VA overcoat to the courthouse to hear plaintiffs and defendants tell various versions of the truth. He also liked to tease his easily humiliated wife by saying there was no use his coming home on a cold winter night when he could stay in a nice warm cell at the jail, or the sheriff's boarding house, as he called it.

Ma kept her wild man's trap stocked with good food when she had anything to cook, and she could make something good out of most anything. She was proud to see Pa tuck away three dozen pancakes at a sitting or a whole pie, but it hurt her that at the same time he could describe as incomparable the flavor of coffee cooked in a tin can over a hobo fire. She enjoyed his hearty laugh and didn't mind that he drove around the countryside asking for old magazines and windfall apples, but she would always have preferred that he be better turned out. When he prepared for a Veteran's Rally or a Decoration Day parade, she boiled and flat-ironed his white shirt, chased us kids out doors so we wouldn't make him nervous for his weekly shave, clipped the hairs from his ears and nostrils and draped his watch chain over his size fifty-two chest. Then with a lonesome tear or two she would watch him walk away to fellowship and spirited exchanges about how to manipulate Uncle.

My mother seldom went along. Strictly a white glove type of lady for trips away from home, she never had the right clothes and she said her English wasn't good enough. Except for the five annual birthday celebrations with her sisters and school affairs that featured one of us kids, Ma's chief pleasure was the prolonged supper hour around the lamplit dining table when she told stories about her childhood in Germany and single blessedness in Cleveland. As long as we could keep her talking, the later we could put off washing the greasy dishes.

Perhaps I should have called them milky dishes, for milk was the stand-by of our lives. When you ask a modern kid if he wants a glass of milk and he asks you if it's cold, I'd like to hit him on his pamper. Milk is always cold today. It never has a chance to be anything else as they rush it from udder to cooler through refrigerated pipes. Back in the twenties it was a different story. We never had complaints against milk of any temperature. It was good squirted directly from the Jersey cow into a tin cup, and we drank it all warm and foamy. It was delicious a little cooler when we dipped it out of flat pans that we kept on the square grand piano in the front room. That was the north side of the house. Lake Erie was only four miles away, remember; so it was the logical place to keep milk, and we drank it by the quart with cinnamon kuchen or apple pie. Milk was out of this world turned into creamy cottage cheese or custard pie, and when the cow was dry, it was even wonderful sucked through tiny little holes in little tin cans. There wasn't very much of that, and we would fight for the chance to carry it to the piano for safe-keeping. Milk was good any old way at all. My mother even liked it when a summer thunderstorm mysteriously turned it thick before it soured.

Our folkways were crude and primitive.

We were just a handful of poor and ugly families living on a road that was called Bloody Run. We never thought of calling the stream of water, that ran along beside the road through the buttercups and stick-tites, a rivulet or a brook. It was a plain old ditch and it supplied all our water except what we caught in barrels under the eaves when it rained. We Crawfords weren't buddy-buddy with all our neighbors, but we did share a common dread that the ditch might run dry. We also shared a common dream, that the Illuminating Company might run a power line down our way. Twice, by some miracle, the light company got so close to granting this boon that my father went out and borrowed a hundred dollars to pay his assessment for the poles. Both times the project fell through. They have lights there now, but the boys and girls who grew up on Bloody Run have long since hitched their way out to jobs that would earn them root-beer and bathtubs.

Thirteen was the proper age for the girls to find jobs washing other people's dishes and diapering their babies. The boys had to wait a few years before they could hire out at the Rubber Works or sign onto the lake freighters in the spring. All of us jumped homeward across the ditch singing if we had money in our pockets, bringing treats for the homefolks. But when the snooty ladies didn't like the way the girls dusted under the beds or the boys got seasick on the lake, we slouched home penniless, glad to have a mess of boiled potatoes and milk gravy.

We had some slightly odd neighbors. There was one small woman tyrant who worked so hard that she cursed her rugs when she beat them, and kicked her sons out of bed to go feed the chickens and clean out the barn. There was old Mr. Drummond who couldn't bear to waste a thing, not even sawdust. He never cut up the logs for the kitchen stove, but let them stick out clear across the floor, and he would cackle happily as he watched his wife and kids jump over the logs as they went about their work. There was a Mrs. Quag who never really wanted to be anything but an old maid, but she didn't know how to say no when some brash young man wanted to marry her.

Mrs. Quag came up to our house fretting one day because her four year old was ailing. "I hate to spend the money on a doctor," she complained. "What do you think I should do? When you've had a kid around for four years, you kinda hate to lose him."

Then there was the Baker, our neighbor to the east. A pale doughy woman, her hands were always at their best on baking days when she whacked up an applesauce cake, two–three pies, a batch of sour-cream cookies and a pan of biscuits. After each cookie sheet or bread pan was slid triumphantly into her oven or onto a rack to cool, the Baker would pick her way around the brush piles and mud puddles to come over and tell us all about it.

"You know that little blue bowl of mine. Wal, I had that about two thirds full of sour cream; so I beat in a coupla duck eggs and a pinch of salt and a nubbin of nutmeg—"

Each recipe was good for half an hour, but the greatest fun she got out of baking was the cruel game she played with her little hen-pecked husband and their child whom she called The Kid. Whenever she sank breathlessly into one of our golden-oak chairs with her whole face grinning, it was to report on her latest skirmish.

"And I sez, 'No, ye cannot have any of that elderberry pie. Who do ye think ye are? I'm saving that because one of my sisters might drop it. No, you ain't a gonna have one of them biscuit. I baked them to have them on hand. Bread will have to do ye."

By midweek, if her sisters had not come, she might let them have a piece of dry cake or soggy pie, and when they refused the lot, she brought it to us. My mother always thanked her but set it out for the chickens as soon as the Baker turned her back to plod home. Milton insisted that the Baker was too lazy to wash her pans, and she'd stop bringing us her garbage if we'd return the utensils dirty, but my mother was too polite for that. There wasn't anything polite about Milton. He'd mimic the Baker to her face unless my mother drove him out to chop wood.

There was one well-to-do family on the street. They owned a hundred acres, kept ice in their ice-box all summer, and their daughter took piano lessons. They never seemed to enjoy life much. Mother and daughter were dainty and clean, but old Steve lunged through work days of no less than seventeen hours until he was too tired to say more than "Co-boss" to the Holsteins. Daughter Elizabeth had so little scope for her talents that she played teacher on the school bus, and when the big boys wouldn't behave she'd hit them with her lunch bucket. You'd never think when you saw her playing a lady teacher that her father looked like a disgruntled bull as he walked, and often smelled like a wet sheep.

But then none of us smelled like roses. Water pumped from the well in the front yard and lugged through the house to be heated on the oil stove was hard and scummy. The rainwater was better if it was fresh, but it soon got full of wigglers. We had to treasure every basin of water. In the summer if we had money for gas and the flivver was running, we took our baths in Lake Erie. In the winter sometimes the well froze and it was hard to get enough to wash dishes, let alone clothes or bodies.

My parents never spanked their children. If you have an immigrant's appreciation of what a child can become, and still are so poor that you have to scrounge for food, and yet succeed in raising every child fairly healthy, you may agree with my mother that children are too precious to be beaten. Of course, if a boy was too mouthy, a tongue lashing never hurt. My father did once raise his heavy hand against one of us,—I don't need to say which one—when the out-house seemed too far away and the kid urinated on the upstairs bedroom floor right over the kitchen table where Pa was eating fried eggs, but that was the exception.

They never pushed education either, but their bragging about every educational advance we made increased our efforts. Margaret had such beautiful handwriting she became the official letter writer. Milton could understand the directions about how to put the furnace together when it came through the mail, and I knew what a lot of the puzzling big words meant. We were surrounded constantly with reading material, thanks to my father, who never got past the fourth grade. The window seat was always stuffed and over-flowing with magazines he cadged all over town. He only read Westerns and adventure pulps himself, as he leaned back in his swivel chair and protected his eyes with a green celluloid eye-shade. We sometimes thought it was the glare of the setting sun over the rocky mountains he was shutting out. The oil lamp wasn't that bright.

Ma preferred newspapers, especially the stories that were serialized. She read us So Big, and The Little Shepherd of Kingdom Come by installments from the Painesville Telegraph. I learned to read before I went to school by looking at the funnies, and I can still remember my mother's surprised wide eyes when I showed her that I recognized the name of Krazy Kat.

At the time, I thought we didn't have any refinements, no capital C culture of any kind, but now I can remember how my mother sang when she was happy. "Daisy, Daisy, give me your answer true. I'm half crazy, over the love of you. It won't be a stylish marriage. We can't afford a carriage, but you'll look sweet upon the seat of a bicycle built for two."

She also sang The Lorelei and something called Roslein Rot, and there was another that I've never found anywhere that went: "Cowbells are ringing in sleepy land, Bye-lo, bye-eye-lo. Cowbells are ringing in sleepy land for Mary, Molly and me."

The kind of lady who said she would rather be beaten than sworn at (and you may be sure that no one ever beat her), a woman who detested vulgarity, there was still one time when my mother lost all her refinement. She had become fond of our black horse and was almost brave enough to try hitching her to the buggy so she could go somewhere by herself, when Pa came home with the piebald result of his latest trade. Ma was so mad she threw a frying pan straight through the window at Pa's head when he came up the back walk. Pa returned it to her with a bow and a patient smile, revealing to our unbelieving eyes a touch of the upper-class Scottish ancestor Pa hoped he resembled.

That was Pa's one affectation. When he really wanted to impress a stranger, say an affluent looking character who stopped to ask his way to Mentor Beach, or someone who wanted to hire a berry picker, Pa would include in his talk so many words like twa and maun and a-weel that we would blush at his pretentiousness. We knew he thought he sounded like Harry Lauder or Robert Burns.

With both my parents astonishing me by stepping out of character at times, I thought I learned early in life not to have any illusions, but my whole life has been one discovery after another. One of my preschool certainties was that I would never say no to food anywhere or anytime, and yet one day at age nine, when my mother had to scrape the flour bin for enough thickening for the milk gravy, I set a whole rhubarb pie the Baker had brought us out for the chickens.

Another stronger conviction was that I hated brothers. I couldn't feel anything else when Milton would hold up my doll by her feet to prove to me she wasn't alive. "You think she's real, don't you, you dumbbell. Fine. I'm going to hang her up in a pear tree so the blood will rush to her head and she'll die."

Or when he said, "You're such a stupe you thought they were laughing at your jokes. All the time they were laughing about the holes in your stockings and the way your ragged slip hung down."

Or: "Do me a favor when we get to town, huh? Walk on the other side of the street. I don't like to lead a parade of elephants."

Or when he said to Margaret, "A guy at school was telling me you seemed to think he was going to ask you for a date. He was only waiting until you shut your trap so he could tell you there was a hair in your mouth."

How could I help hating brothers when I had that kind? And yet there was a bewildering episode when I was four, and my mother told me we were going to have another baby. I prepared for a little sister with every scrap of magic and prayer I could muster. I named the unborn baby Charlotte, and stuffed all the little boy caps and suits under the attic floor on the theory that a boy wouldn't come if there were no clothes ready for him. I refused to consider any kind of baby but a girl.

Then one night my father herded the three of us upstairs at a ridiculously early hour and instead of going to bed, we huddled on the landing listening to all the mysterious flurry below. Eventually we were summoned by a proud announcement. Pa knew all the time we were wide awake.

"All right, you kids. You can come down now and see your new baby brother."

Crushed with disappointment, a sob in my aching throat, I still wanted to see him. He was something new even if his personality would be all wrong, and there in a washbasket I found an adorable baby, his hair the downy yellow of new baby chick, his eyes a deep blue in a sleepy pink face. He was everything a baby ought to be. It was a priceless moment in which I was given a reprieve from the burden of hating brothers, a moment that cleaned and sweetened the air in a widening circle. I was delightfully mistaken about something, and I didn't have to take responsibility for managing the obstreperous world. Even Milt looked good to me.

Although Ben grew up to be a Wallace supporter, the moment of his becoming my little brother is still precious.

RELATIVES

3

All my high school friends were extraordinary. Alice could play Humoresque on the piano, Millie could sink a basket ball through the hoop most any time she tried, and Jean had once spent a winter with her family at White Sulphur Springs. Barbara's dresses were the latest style, fitting so closely at the bust that our Home Ec teacher had to warn us that there were women in the world, and she had devoutly hoped we would never know any, who liked, actually liked, showing their shapes.

For years my sister and I couldn't find anything to brag about. When everyone else carried a pretty lunch box with a thermos, we sacked unwrapped jelly bread sandwiches, pinching off little chunks inside the bag so the girls wouldn't know we didn't have waxed paper. We couldn't talk about movie stars knowingly because we never went to the movies, and we couldn't perform musically at the school assemblies. I tried hard to make people laugh by repeating jokes I'd overheard in the berry patch or the feed store, but that never got me more than polite smiles.

About mid-way through the tenth grade, Marge discovered that we had one item in our "Hey-look-at-me" repertoire that was a natural winner, and from that time on we played it big. We had cousins, thirty-two living and eight passed on, a vigorous and exciting bunch dead or alive, who dwarfed our friends' puny family connections. We even had romantic unknown cousins, the children of my mother's half brother and sister, who had escaped to England from Germany so that Uncle Gottlieb could dodge the forced German military service. There was also the pathetic story of my father's nieces, little lost Sally and Marie, who had been snatched by a wicked welfare department when their parents were down on their luck.

Our cousins Willy and Wally with the rascally grins and the ragged hair could swing from the trees like Tarzan. Our tall cousin Paul and our refined cousin Helen were graduating from college, and Karl was already getting by-lines on his newspaper sports stories. It sounded ever so much classier to say that we couldn't stay for the football game or attend the Hard Times dance because we didn't want to miss seeing our cousins at Aunt Pauline's birthday party or cousin Mathilda's wedding, than to admit we didn't have the money for tickets. It sounded fairly important too to tell how much we were needed to watch cousin Anna's darling little children, Billy and Bunny, while Anna canned tomatoes on her farm down Middlefield way.

We didn't have any boy-friends, but we had a handsome cousin Eddie and a daring cousin Clyde who was in the Navy and had learned all about French kissing on one of his trips to see the world. And we were very lucky girls to have our coats handed down from cousins Martha and the sophisticated Freda. They wore only the nicest things, and they really took care of their clothes too, hangers in the closet every time.

For tragedy we could tell about the sad death of our lovely and saintly cousin Lina of influenza (a beautiful word). We didn't remember Lina but that didn't detract from her legend. For comedy, we told about our red-haired cousin Florence, the giggling girl who could josh other hapless motorists into changing her flat tires and who once induced an innocent salesman to push her gasless rattletrap six homeward miles by telling him she was sure it only needed one more little jolt before the motor would catch. The fact that the German relatives had grand rolling names like Heimerdinger, Finkemeier, and Keyerleber perked up the accounts.

In later years I became disillusioned about the lasting quality of borrowed glory, but Margaret went right on discovering precious ore in the family mine. Any time you have a week off she can show you her nuggets, and demonstrate convincingly that each strike is so productive she must go on to second, third, and fourth cousins as well as to by-gone generations.

Our maternal grandparents died long before my mother became an American; so we never knew them, and the Crawford grandparents we didn't think were worth mentioning until Margaret began her research. Grandpa, as the youngest child of an adoring mother, hadn't been allowed to go to school so he grew up illiterate and unskilled. With nothing to offer a bride except his not very illustrious name, Grandpa reckoned that would be a good enough bargaining point when he heard about a girl in the next township who had been tossed out of her home for producing an unexpected child. His whole family laughed when Grandpa rented a livery rig and set off to find him a wife, and Grandpa himself could hardly believe his good fortune when Grandma Clarissa said she would have him. When I knew Grandma, she'd already had ten more children and fifty years of wedded poverty. She was a grim little lady, every inch of her covered in black except for her face and hands, and I wish she had lived long enough to hear the flabbergasting history of her forbears that Magaret turned up. I think Grandma had herself forgotten that she had once been a member of a renowned and respectable pioneer family, descended from Revolutionary War colonists, because her sources of pride in late life had narrowed down to reeling off the birth-dates of all her grandchildren and striking the biceps of her son Ezra when he teased too much.

Grandpa as an old man still had the flavor of the sweet and trusting child who'd been unable to stand up to a domineering mother. Although I was a great big lunk of a girl when he made his one visit to us, I pretended that I was afraid to jump across the ditch. I'd heard that grandfathers were supposed to have some such kindly helping function, and Grandpa did not fail me. He got me across safely and then fell in himself, and Grandma explained to him all the rest of the day in sharp clear language like hammer blows that he was a clumsy, stupid fool who should have known better.

Grandpa's great ambition in life was to learn to tell time and to own a team of mules. He didn't make it, but one of his devilish sons sent him a telegram that his mules were arriving on the next passenger train and Grandpa ran all the way to the depot and searched through the alighting crowd for a couple pair of long hairy ears.

Margaret can tell you too about hefty Henrietta whose dainty ankles snapped when her weight passed three hundred and sixty, and about long-footed Lulu who had to go barefoot after some nefarious burglar stole her specially constructed size thirteens. The story I dearly prize is about freckle faced, five year old Tad, whose mother told him to stay in their broken down car and watch the baby when she went for help. When the mother returned the road where she had left her little family was empty, but there was a dim blur a mile or so farther down under a shady tree.

When worried Mama caught up with her little darling and inquired how he had arrived at that spot, little Tad piped up, "I started her up. What the hell did you think I was going to do? Sit there in the hot sun?"

Margaret claims he grew up to be a famous evangelist.

My sister made it a practice to write to relatives whether they answered or not. For twenty years she sent yearly letters to Uncle Walter, who had somehow made his fortune in the gold rush although he couldn't possibly have reached California until several decades too late. We also believed that he had retired to some mountain stronghold and lived there alone with Rin-Tin-Tin. Some of our aunts and uncles said he'd probably died long ago and good riddance because he'd never been anything but a cranky bugger, but Margaret kept right on writing on the simple principle that every human being likes to get a little mail now and then.

One fall morning she was roused by a stranger's voice calling from California.

"I just put your uncle Walter on the eastbound train. He has a bad heart, probably can't live very long, and he says he wants to see you before he dies. He asked me to let you know so you could meet him at the Nickel Plate Depot."

Margaret uh-huhed and thank-youed, half believing this was another long distance dastardly trick of the far flung Crawford cousins. They had been known to send unsigned telegrams with directions to start the flapjacks because six were arriving for breakfast. She met the train, though, on the off chance it was no joke, and recognized for a Crawford the little old fellow who shakily stepped down with a "By God, I made it," look in his eye. They got along fine. He said he hated the whole damn family except her and he had embarked on this perilous journey so he could know his heiress. When his old heart failed a few years later, he really did leave her his life savings, five little houses, and a tract of desert land near Las Vegas.

Now Marge has several more correspondents, all of whom once lived in those five little houses: the railroad widow who is buying the place in Colton, some Italian family in Maryland who sublet the house in Loma Linda, and the veteran who fell off the roof of the house in San Berdoo and hurt his back. There's also Uncle's old friend McNabb who is having it so rough with his third wife. Unquestionably, Margaret will benefit from all these relationships. She always does.

A grateful old age recipient she befriended left her his whole estate, which came in handy. She was able to give each cousin an imitation diamond stick-pin for Christmas and she found a good home for the bed pan. She has won a blue ribbon at the fair with a do-hickey fashioned by some old lady's arthritic fingers. It makes a nice addition to Margaret's jelly roll and angel food cake masterpieces. In fact, she acquired so many blue ribbons that she made them into a pillow cover and won another blue ribbon.

Her profits might not be financial. Marge is quite happy with dividends in humor. There was a little ragged half-wit who shambled through town with her quarter-wit son. Margaret hunted through her rummage for a nice dress and coat because it hurt her to see poor Bessie so ragged. Bessie was grateful for the garments in a spirited, condescending way.

Hitching her skinny frame to a fancier stance, Bessie proclaimed, "I think they might just do when I go out dancing with my boy friend."

Margaret laughed for a week. "It was like she was sorry for me, spending my time at rummage sales when she had much more fun dating. Can you picture the kind of guy who would take old Bessie out? The poor thing probably invented him."

Bessie may not have known that Marge had a boy friend of her own. For fifteen years Ray helped Marge pack picnic baskets to take along to Headlands beach. They both loved to bid on cream pitchers and discarded photographs of other folks' ancestors at auctions, inspect Poland China hogs and fancy work at county fairs, and listen to Harry Lauder and John McCormack on old wax recordings. Better than anything they enjoyed park benches and idling along Main Street where they could observe the funny world go by. Ray thought most women ridiculously fussy worriers who missed out on the larger values. Twisting his rotund face into a sour grimace, he shifted into the role of Miss Small Town Old Maid.

"I haven't slept a wink since the shade began flapping around three-thirty-nine this morning. I knew the time because I'd been in just a little light doze since half an hour after midnight when I had to get up for a glass of luke warm water with lemon juice. My stomach is so edgy, and I had this sharp pain right over the pancreas. I'll bet it was that slice of cucumber I had for supper. Cucumber will do it every time. Raspberries will too."

Ray was something of an expert on old maids because he was pretty fussy himself. He hated insensitive boorishness in men as well as the triviality of silly women; so he lived alone in a clean and tidy house with his dachshund Fritzie. He seemed to have everything worked out to his own satisfaction, so we were all thunderstruck when he asked Marge to marry him. She believed he was serious when he stopped at the doctor's office for a blood test. Very touched and pleased then, Margaret put on a clean blue and white checked gingham and they went over to the minister's study to be married.

Nine months later Ray was dead, fading away along with his interest in life, refusing medical care and food. Margaret understands now that he must have known his life was about finished and that he married her to leave her a little better off with his National Service Life Insurance. She needed the help more than his relatives, and she had been his dearest friend, but it must have been a tremendous psychological cost to him for he had never been a marrying man.

All twenty of my aunts and uncles are gone now except Aunt Olive, the one with the thick, luxurious wavy hair that once earned her living for her when she sat in a store window advertising shampoo. She is eighty now and her hair is still brilliantly glossy and her laughter is still rich. Aunt Olive lives in a wheel chair now, but that didn't stop her from falling in love by telephone with another wheelchair patient two years back, and she has written me vividly about their romance.

Uncle John was one of the first to leave us. He was the one that had some kind of fits in childhood and nobody thought he would live to grow up; he turned out to be such a beautiful dancer that he was able to marry three times, and every one of his wives was too good for him, the family insisted. Uncle John had goals which were unusual for his time, one of which was to ridicule the respectable life. He was terrific in his idiot act, full of gibbering meaningful nonsense. Then he loved to tell about the summer he posed as a famous tree surgeon and charged gullible Hoosiers exorbitant prices to fasten fly paper around their stately elms. I can still hear him describe to one of my gullible aunts how to make soup from the belly feathers of a Plymouth Rock hen. Uncle

John counted each day lost that he had not fooled someone.

He could be a little mean sometimes too. Once he appeared at our house loaded down with ripe bananas and announced, "I always wanted to see if I could eat a whole peck." Before our envious eyes he did just that without offering us a bite.

For a short time Uncle John was a chauffeur for a wealthy financier who didn't like to waste time on his way to the office. Uncle John enjoyed getting the most out of a Caddy himself, but one morning he had such a hang-over, he could hardly see the road so he was taking it easy, and the back-seat aristocrat complained. Deliber-ately then Uncle John headed for the biggest chuck hole he could find and the impact bounced the employer so hard against the roof of the car that his high silk hat was whacked down over his face as far as his mustache, and Uncle John laughed so hard he had to pull over to the curb and roll in the grass. For some reason he lost his job that day.

We missed Uncle John terribly when he died.

Although completely without guile, Uncle Ezra was equally eccentric. Living alone in untidy ease, he fed the countless cats that wandered in and out, and he became a checker champion by practicing with a young tabby he taught to play opposite. If the puzzled puss hesitated too long, Uncle Ezra would unselfishly guide the velvet paw to the next move. He kindly accepted whatever was offered to him, including marriage to a divorcee with two bed-wetting children, but when she decided that she preferred a neighbor, he was just as contented to have her move down the block. All his time was spare except for odd-job carpentry, and he fiddled for fun on home-made violins. In his old age Uncle Ezra became a little more peculiar, and one day the neighbors had to call the police when they saw the old man sitting on the front steps pouring red paint over his head. They carried him away to the state hospital for a few weeks, until the paint wore off. I've always wondered what he had in mind.

Uncle Dave was the one Crawford who could have fit well into my mother's side of the family; he still had a zest for the bizarre, but in him it was a sweet natured appreciation that life held a variety of possibilities for good. As a youth he learned that there was money in buying big bottles of vanilla, dividing the contents into little bottles and selling them to country housewives. With the flavoring proceeds, he supported nine children who loved and admired their father throughout his vigorous life. Four of his sons became clergymen. In his nineties Uncle Dave was still the love ideal of older women in Tampa, Florida, after fifty years of happy married life to the three wives who died before him.

The cousins are disappearing one by one too, but among their fifty-four offspring are still enough relatives for lively family reunions, the good old fashioned cooks contributing the sort of baked beans, potato salad, and apple pies that keep the family circling the table for more. Some of the staid Ohio relatives still think that all babies should have blue eyes. But a few tradition breaking youngsters are shaking the family tree. One boy who went into the Peace Corps married a Yap Island native in a grass skirt. When I attend a family get-together, I am always surprised that there are still so many blonde children being reproduced, and about how much I still like my cousins.

RICH FOLKS

4

Never knowing any rich people, I built some lovely illusions about them from society pages and library books. They never discussed constipation, called their neighbors names, or chased bedbugs. Their library shelves reached to the ceiling and you could climb a little ladder on a track for a copy of David Copperfield or Graustark. You could also read all night by electricity instead of by the dwindling coal oil while you raced to find out if the lovers' lips ever met in a kiss. Rich people never walked barefoot on the straw stubbles, waded through a sea of mud to the outhouse, or screamed with blasting pain because what they thought was a rain hat turned out to be a wasp colony. For a long time after I was fourteen when my sister told me about human conception, I still believed that rich people like ministers reproduced by sleeping peacefully together instead of acting like animals, but by the time I had the wondrous chance to share a home with the wealthy, I knew better than that.

At eighteen I hailed the interstate Greyhound in Mentor, Ohio. The driver stowed my cornflake carton luggage underneath, and I climbed aboard to "take a position" as maid in New York. Marge had been there for a few months and had found a place for me. She explained that I would be paid five dollars a week plus my room and board and would be able to learn how to keep a nice house looking good. Naturally, I couldn't turn that down. Mr. and Mrs. Byrd were kindly paying my fare on faith that I would work it out.

"They must be awfully nice people to do that," I told the man with the blackheads who sat beside me.

He said, "Yeah," and fumbled for my knee.

I raved on brightly. "I can't wait to have a pretty room. We finally got some beaver board put up where my sister and I sleep, and when the roof leaked the rain made sort of interesting patterns running down, but it wasn't pretty. They say I'll even have a private bath."

For some reason he avoided me at the stopover in Scranton, but I didn't care because the closer we got to New York City the more I felt like a member of the Byrd family who didn't need the companionship of strangers. The New York bus station was disconcerting with its abundant evidence that poverty was not confined to Ohio. I tried to overlook the toothless mother feeding a litter of sticky kids on hamburgers and chocolate bars. I gave up my place on a bench to a hag whose swollen feet were bursting through the bunion windows of her broken shoes. I refused to repent and be saved to please a squint eyed gnome who poked pamphlets in my face. Where in that smelly crowd was Mrs. Byrd? Another derelict approached and I brushed her aside, but she persisted in wanting my attention. She wore a soup spotted butt-sprung knit dress. Greasy straight hair dangled half way between her silly ear bobs and her skinny neck bones, framing an off-white face with red smeared lips, and Oh-my-God! She was asking if I were Ellen.

This couldn't be Mrs. Byrd!

It was.

I didn't have any money to go back home. Heavy heart scrunching down into the corner of my empty stomach, I hoisted my luggage by its dress belt binders and followed the scarecrow, telling myself that Marge had said this was a good job and she couldn't be this far wrong. Maybe the lady was eccentric about the way she dressed, but threw her money around on food. She'd probably stop at some nice restaurant and invite me to shoot the works.

She didn't.

But how she did talk! All the way to New Rochelle in the sputtering Oldsmobile, it was all about Bridie, that incomparable Irish maid who had just left for unclear reasons after seventeen years, her tearful departure spreading the shamrock carpet of good luck for me. I was such a lucky girl to follow in Bridie's footsteps!

"Bridie had such a clever system of keeping everything looking nice. On Monday mornings she would put the clothes to soak before breakfast and then she'd whisk around the living room while the muffins were baking, and then she'd have the clothes on the line in no time after washing the dishes and tidying the kitchen. Do you like children? Bridie just loved our Miss Flopsie and Mr. Goose and she practically brought up Miss Mopsie. The children would do anything for her when they were little. Miss Flopsie is seventeen now and an accomplished pianist. Mr. Goose is interested in history. Was your mother in service too?"

"Was she what? Oh, you mean—, well, no, not since she got married."

And another bubble burst. Did this creep with the dirty neck think I had any intention of living out my life as a servant? Could she possibly imagine that our family cherished traditions of being floor mopping retainers?

"I hope you like dogs. Bridie just loved our three."

Dogs? Oh, sure, dogs. Friendly pals of the farm and woods. Were there people who didn't like dogs?

"Well, that's nice, because we have raised them from puppies. Genevieve is the oldest. She was just five in March. Maxine and Adrian are her children. They are WIRE HAIRED TERRIERS."

Her pride in ownership of that particular breed was a fine thing to behold. Not being acquainted with what I assumed must be some wise and gentle St. Bernard type pawshaker, I glowed along with her.

"Bridie was crazy about dogs. And she was such a comfort to Allys. She knew just how to fix his morning coffee and she did all those little extra things like whipping up little cakes and making tasty stews from leftovers. Allys was always so fond of Bridie's chocolate bread pudding."

Allys? He? Who in the world was Allys? I was so confused, I had to say it.

"I thought you were Allys."

"How odd that you should think that, as if I would ever sign my first name to a business letter. My husband is Allys, of course."

We careened around a corner and I fell against the car door, which gave me time to straighten my face. Was that the kind of name a rich man wore? Where I came from, men were Pete and Joe and Ed. We had a Lum once, but no male named Allys could have survived.

Mrs. Byrd prattled on about how funny it must be to live way out in Ohio on the prairies. She'd come from Rye herself of a fine old family. Her great uncle was a Lieutenant Commander who had distinguished himself in some Spanish American battle. I told her that my father was in that war too.

Mrs. Byrd wasn't impressed. "A private, no doubt. You can see that I have a great deal to be proud of in my family. You know that Allys is an architect. Oh, you don't? I supposed your sister would have told you. I understand from Mrs. Branem, your sister's employer, that your mother came from Germany. Allys was pleased to hear that because he says that Germans are so thorough, he was sure you'd had good training."

It was coming through pretty strong that this snob thought of herself as something so special that she could look down on Marge and me and our family as low class morons not really fit to do her dirty work although there might be some redeeming strain in our Teutonic ancestry. Hastily kicking out of sight in my cranial bushes any variety of that idea I might have harbored, I bristled. We were not low class. We were poor, but bright and promising, not like the outfit down the road whose kids always smelled of urine and couldn't learn to read, or like the riff-raff gang who lived, all eighteen of them, in a chicken coop. We always had something to eat and our father had a job sometimes except in the winter. I was about to explain that I planned on college by September, but already I could sense that she would not be pleased. So I said something worse.

"I was wondering why my sister didn't come along for the ride to meet me."

Mrs. Byrd was so startled she almost crashed a crossing gate. I wilted under her lady-like sarcasm. "What a droll idea! This isn't Thursday. I'm sure Margaret wouldn't be so inconsiderate of Mrs. Branem. Would a maid in Ohio suggest such a thing?"

I said that I didn't think they had maids in Ohio, but she wasn't listening. She gave her attention now to turning into the driveway of a mean little house on a plain street that ran along beside the railroad tracks, which was my ignorant term. I learned later that rich people never, never live by the tracks although it is acceptable for their houses to be near "the railroad right of way." I suppose the Byrd's steep frame house on its narrow lot was better than our place back home, but it was nowhere as pretty or as well kept as the homes of some of my friends. As Mrs. Byrd squeezed the car into its hole under the house, a frenzy of shrill barking greeted us from the railed porch above the garage. Just as I left the car, fifteen pounds of squealing wire haired pedegree vaulted the barricade and plopped practically on my head.

Dropping her bag in the dust, Mrs. Byrd tore apart her crimson lips in a scream. "Catch her! Catch her, Stupid! She'll run away."

Too flabbergasted to do anything but stand there like a hick, I watched Mrs. Byrd scramble after her darling whom she breathlessly introduced to me later as Genevieve, the pride of the household, so brilliant that she could jump off the porch while Maxine and Adrian could only bark. It was a great thrill. I was about to take a tip from Genevieve and run away myself, when a little girl dashed out, soft brown hair falling from a silver barrette, shoe laces flapping, a nice, everyday smile of welcome on her plain little face. This was Mopsie, a lovable unspoiled nine year old.

Mopsie showed me the house. I felt more miserable with each lagging step. The living room was so small that it was over-crowded with one chair plus the baby grand piano.

"See the fireplace," Mopsie offered. "Bridie spent most of her time polishing the brass handles of the tools. You'll use the shovel all the time to clean up after the dogs."

Everywhere was neglect, dust, dirty windows and broken down furniture. The kitchen groaned under its load of dirty dishes that apparently no one had touched since Bridie departed. Assorted trash slid from the open cupboard doors. The hallway was barely passable, the stairway carpet dangerously ragged. Mopsie took my hand.

"You can see the upstairs later. I'll show you your room."

That idea cheered me. "At least I'll have a bathroom," I consoled myself. "That's better than what I had before."

Little did I know!

Mrs. Byrd came along probably to hear me coo with delight, any room of her own automatically being heaven for a girl of my class from way out west. When on first sight I only looked sick, for this was the grubbiest room of all, Mrs. Byrd kindly said that I could spend an hour getting settled before starting dinner. Mopsie helped me turn the two foot wide couch around so that I could sleep in the angle of the broken springs and the wall and she volunteered to find a wash cloth. Rag was the word for what she brought me, a sour gray, wet thing.

"I had to bring you mine," Mopsie apologized. "There aren't any others so I'll share with Flopsie."

Behind narrow double doors in the wall I found, not the expected clothes closet, but my very own private bath. It was in two sections. Never having lived in a house so luxuriously fitted, I tried not to be critical of those two slots of blistered metal. I could see that if I squeezed into the right-hand slot in a jack-knife position, I could with only minor difficulty slide under the rusty wash-bowl which overlapped the toilet. Having used the bus station facilities, I could wait for that experience. What I wanted immediately was a bath.

After dusting out the cobwebs in the left-hand shower slot with my handkerchief, and removing my bus-mussed clothing, I reached in to turn on the water. It was very rusty and not hot either, but I didn't think I could afford to be fussy. Knocking off no more than half a pound of ancient flaking paint as I sidled carefully in, I soon understood that this angled tin can would have made a fine coffin for an upright starvation victim. I could fit in all right even with the door shut, but I had never starved, and there obviously wasn't room for me to raise my arms to wash myself. I wriggled out, lathered myself copiously, and then wedged in again to rinse under the stubborn tepid trickle. It was my first shower, and it felt good. I didn't know that the water level wasn't supposed to rise above my ankles and I stood there dreamily until there was a sharp metallic bang on the door and the equally metallic tones of Mrs. Byrd.

"Would you please not use the shower? The drain doesn't work and it makes the plaster fall off the garage ceiling onto the car. Allys doesn't like that. Anyway, it's time to start dinner."

I wish now I had gone out the way I was.

In the kitchen the whole family was assembled to view their new apparatus, me. I had thought that Flopsie and I might be friends since we were about the same age, but she was a discontented pouter and her greeting was a chilly, "I do wish you would dust the piano keys, Ellen. They are so dirty I can't practice."

Nobody before or since has ever said my name in quite that way, indicating so precisely the place I was to occupy. At once I became a Thing.

Goose, the fourteen year old heir of the family fortune, God help him!, was a rangy broad shouldered boy with a whiny voice. He didn't bother with me but leaned against the sink complaining, "Mother-r-r, where were you when school was out? I had to walk the whole mile home. When will dinner be ready?"

Later I understood why Goose had no strength. He never had enough to eat. I was instructed to divide a can of tuna fish, two tomatoes, and a half head of lettuce for the six of us. My brother, Ben, a picky eater, would have considered that a taste. He used a quart of milk and a half dozen slices of homemade bread with peanut butter and jelly for a snack. Goose, poor fellow, never had such luck.

But the great personality in that dingy kitchen was Allys. Nothing girlish about him. Allys reacted with a man's loud voice and a man's temper to a world in which everything was against him. I couldn't blame him much. He lived in squalid discomfort with a gone-to-seed wife, a whimpering son, and a supercilious daughter. He never made any money. Mopsie might have been a comfort to him, but all he ever noticed about her was that she hadn't combed her hair. Now the poor fellow had the worst affliction of all, an untrained maid. I didn't even know how to make chocolate bread pudding.

On my first memorable day with the filthy rich, Mrs. Byrd allowed me to visit my sister after nine in the evening. I was uncertain whether to hug Marge, or slap her for getting me into this fix, when she met me at her back step and quietly closed the door behind her. She was carrying a paper bag and this was the reason for stealth.

"Maudie spies on me," she whispered. "I bought us some stale doughnuts last night. If Maudie sees the bag, she'll tell her mother I'm stealing something and Mrs. Branem always says, 'No four year old would lie, Margaret.' Let's buy some coffee at the drugstore and sit on a park bench. Or maybe you've had such a good supper you don't want any more."

"Marge, you devil. You knew what kind of people they are. How could you send for me?"

Margaret laughed. Or perhaps that choking sound was crying. "You wanted to see the world. You said you wanted to travel. I thought we could see New York for a few months and then go home." Tears dripped off her nose. "They're so mean, El, and so stingy. The poorest people in Ohio don't live like this."

I savored every doughnut crumb and licked out the last of the sugared coffee. "And they have the nerve to look down on us, Marge."

"Oh, sure, El. That's all they have to do. I've been watching them for two months now and I'm sure the Byrds don't have any money at all, and the Branems are only a little better off. None of them know how to do a thing in the house. You know what they call a good time? They sit in their cars in the driveway and talk about their maids. They haven't the gas to go riding, but it makes them feel good to order somebody around and then make fun of them."

"Are they all like this, Marge, or did we just happen to get a couple of looloos?"

Marge buttoned her coat against the March wind. "We haven't seen each other for all this time and now we have to visit out in the cold, but I didn't dare ask you to come in. I only know these two families and that's all I want to know."

Too cold to linger, we said good-bye and sought our lumpy beds, probably the only residents in either house who didn't go to sleep hungry that night.

In the following weeks, I delittered the kitchen, evicting a mouse and her babies who had been securely housed in the Dutch oven. I shovelled, mopped, scrubbed, dusted and shovelled again. None of the darling dogs were housebroken. I lost the battle with the piano keys because the rugs were so dirty that any movement set off a whirling dust storm which settled thickly over all ivories, including teeth. After Mrs. Byrd counted the slices of bread in each loaf, the peaches in the can, and the grapes in a bunch, I cooked the rations. Once when Flopsie was away for supper, I ate the sixth bun from Mrs. Byrd's frugal purchase, and she was quite upset all the next day because she'd been drooling in anticipation about that for her lunch. Flopsie, sad little snob, yearned for friends and consulted me hastily one day because she'd been able to bring a man home for lunch from the golf course. Our menu was to be a can of hash dressed out with a can of applesauce and Flopsie decided that would do since we had nothing else, but she asked me to pass finger bowls to add a touch of elegance. The new beau put on a sprightly conversational act. We never saw him again.

Bridie had accomplished her wonders without the aid of appliances. No vacuum, washing machine, or toaster. I pointed out without subtlety that back home we didn't have electricity but we did have a hand powered washer that was better than nothing. They told me that Bridie had never complained; so I continued washing by hand, sheets and all, and hanging them on the rotton clothesline which broke twice every Monday. Then I washed them over again. My point finally got across to Allys, humiliating him to action in somehow finding a used washer and vacuum. The whole family acted just like Ohio peasants in their joy over this evidence that they were coming up in the world.

Cultured Mrs. Byrd didn't seem to know how to wash herself. Every morning while I straightened her ragged bed, Mrs. Byrd worked over her unwashed face with a filthy powder puff, flapping on the talcum as if she were flouring a fish for the skillet. She wore the same unsightly garb every day until the seat threads separated, and her uniform of the next era was equally repulsive. After her afternoon chat with Mrs. Branem, my mentor would regale me with tons of bright hints about how other people's maids could mold pretty salads, keep the windows sparkling, and clean the cupboards,— all before breakfast. I guess the special merit of early morning miracles was to suggest that a good maid didn't sleep.

The lady threw herself into my education as if her place in society depended upon my becoming a proper maid. While I scoured and peeled potatoes, she leaned against the door jamb and read Emily Post in her upperclass voice. I managed to choke back my snickers, until she came to the part about how each piece of silverware should be placed in the dishwater by itself, lest a fork scratch a knife. Then she stalked away huffily, declaring that she didn't see any reason to train me if I didn't appreciate her time and trouble, and she couldn't understand why my mother hadn't told me these things.

I really was a lousy student in her finishing school. Somehow I could not remember to call the children Miss or Mr., and I always failed to identify myself as the maid when I answered the phone. That really hurt Mrs. Byrd. Here she was sacrificing five dollars a week for prestige and getting no mileage out of it. I always thought I'd earned my money by the time Allys snarled his way through breakfast of three stewed prunes and a skimpy piece of toast. He didn't have any jam, but he always spread sarcasm thickly over all the other household members because we weren't energetic, ambitious, and thorough. He wasn't aware how ambitiously I was attacking my own educational project of teaching Mopsie all about democracy and loving one's fellow. She was an eager pupil and had unlimited study time since no one else paid her any attention, except finally, Mrs. Branem, who pointed out how unsuitable it was for the little girl to spend so much time with a servant. Suddenly when school was over, Mopsie was scooped off to a relative for re-indoctrination. When she returned, the ingenuous friendliness was gone. She sometimes sneaked into the kitchen or my room for a few words, but it was clear that she knew it wasn't a nice thing to do.

Marge called one morning to say that she was going home. She'd decided that if she was going to slave at housework for practically nothing, she might as well work for our mother. I stayed until I had saved a hundred dollars and then announced that I was leaving to begin college. Mrs. Byrd was shocked. Why in the world did I want to leave such a nice job when I was just beginning to catch on, she wanted to know. She and Allys had been planning to give me a raise, providing Allys got the contract he'd bid for, and she thought I was happy to be in New York where there was so much to do and see on my day off.

Well, I sat in my mouldy room and thought that over. Yes, there were those grand Thursdays off. I might never have them again. Thursday was such a treat! All I had to do was clean the upstairs, cook and serve the lunch, wash the dishes, cook the supper and set the table. I nearly always got away by two-thirty. Then when I came home I could wash the dishes which they would pile unscraped all over the kitchen. I would really miss those Thursdays. Besides, as Mrs. Byrd told me, what was the use of college? Thousands of college graduates were fighting to get jobs as elevator operators and waitresses. I knew all that. Here I had security, my little broken bed, my three meals a day and such lovely people to work for!

In the end I left anyway. Fool that I was, I headed back to Ohio with its Guernsey cows and gardens full of tomatoes and cucumbers and all that other crude stuff the lower classes go for.

I've often wondered whether Allys got his contract and whether Flopsie found a man and how Mopsie turned out, but I never heard from any of them again.

5

For the Crawford kids of Bloody Run, despite the holes in our stockings, and the fact that I was hopeless in gym, and such humiliations as having the junior class take up a collection to get my brother Milton a haircut, school was fun clear through from the first grade until the hot summer days of glory when we were given our diplomas.

On the long bus ride home from New York, I faced the fact that I'd had some silly illusions about the wealthy members of our land, but perhaps the Byrd family were a poor sample of affluence. About college I couldn't be mistaken. Everything I'd experienced about rich folks before my trip to New York had been vicarious, but I had twelve years of first hand knowledge about schools, and the possibility that I could be deluded in that area never fluttered close. True nobility, I was certain, flourished in institutions of exalted learning. I would meet brilliant and kindly professors who would respond warmly to my enquiring mind. There would be no pettiness or timidity in assailing the great issues of life. Forever emancipated from housework, the scholar in me busily listed all my previously unanswered questions about life's origin and ending. I also wanted to know about morals, manners, and motivations, such as why my father told dirty jokes and my mother could only pronounce a V when it came in the middle of a word.

Like most 1934 paupers who aspired to college, I had applied all over the country for scholarships, but never believed I'd get one; so I was ecstatic when Hiram College in Ohio wrote that they were giving me this great honor. My mother wasn't surprised. Liberty's torch still blazed in her immigrant memory, and everything wonderful could happen to her American children. She went with me to register and even threw off her shyness to go along into the office. This reserved official was not impressed with my treasured hundred dollar bill. He showed me in writing that I would still need forty dollars in addition to my fund and the scholarship. Forty lousy dollars! It might as well have been forty thousand. My mother was crushed. The lowest spot in her whole career as parent, it made a mockery of all those years of successful contriving to find solutions. She thought college people should help now to make ends meet.

"Sure seems like there ought to be some way," she pleaded.

The official expressed sorrow that I would be unable to use the scholarship money, and we drove sadly home. It was an ideal college too, remote, contemplative, vine covered.

My friend Virgie was leaving shortly for some unknown college in Kentucky, and her father suggested that I ride along. If it was too late for registration, I would have a pleasant trip before seeking another place to wash dishes. Thinking that one college was about the same as another academically, I packed my clothes. Since it was a Christian college and I was a good Christian girl, if I did have a few funny ideas, the kind church people at home assured me that any right college would be glad to have me, and they held a clothing shower in my honor.

At the end of the trip Virgie and I watched eagerly for our first view of the campus. And then we turned numb.

On a weedy little plateau the hot sun beat down on two unadorned cheap buildings of yellow brick and two shoddy houses. In the field beyond among scattered log sheds, a few skinny cows picked at the thistles with a handful of dejected chickens scratching out their sustenance in the cows' wake. It didn't look like a college. Stopping at the first house for directions, we found this to be the office and home of President Raeburn, who greeted us jovially. He was glad to see Virgie, whom he expected, but even more pleased by the arrival of an unplanned registrant. Apparently it was never too late to be admitted. He explained to Virgie's father that we would be perfectly safe in his fatherly care, since his program insured that every girl would return home in June with all the purity with which she enrolled. I wasn't quite sure what he meant; all that seemed important to me at the time was whether my hundred dollars would buy a year of college.

The president's eyes popped. "A hundred dollars. Well, well, well! We'll have to tell the Dean about this."

Shepherding us along to the office-home of the Dean, Mr. Raeburn caroled the glad tidings of my fund, and his excited subordinate bleated with joy as he extended a trembling hand. I signed up for history, religion, music, English, German, and biology. By what I thought was a nice coincidence, Virgie was taking the same courses. Later, more knowledgable students told us that there were no other Freshman courses, and mine was the first cash the impoverished school had seen in many a week. They lived by faith there, a terribly devout bunch, and I was the current answer to prayer.

Poverty was grimly visible in the dormitory dining room where we met with fellow students and faculty for supper that night. With not enough silverware to go around, some of us ate with spoons and others with forks or knives. We had beans, tomatoes and hot biscuits which we could drench with sorghum molasses if we were so indoctrinated. Flies and roaches liberally dotted the tables and walls, but there was a friendly gaiety about it all that I liked. Mr. Raeburn gave thanks for the barrel of cocoa someone had donated, and for the new students. Then he explained date hall.

His voice held all the yearning, solemn tenderness of an evangelist. "This is a Christian college and we are all here together because we love the Lord and want to walk in his footsteps. We expect our students to be fine Christian ladies and gentlemen; so there will be no conversations except at the table, and no courting on this campus. Now we wouldn't want to stand in the way of any young lady and gentleman from knowing each other if they are ready to start up the pathway to holy matrimony; so whenever a couple of you come and ask permission, I'll let you visit with each other in date hall, so long as I can see that you're good for one another. Date hall meets every Monday night from seven to nine. The boys will line up at my house, and the girls here in the dormitory and I'll ask a couple of the professors to lead you over to the school building. You'll be well chaperoned while you're there."

He really meant all that too. Eventually I tried that type of dating, intoxicated when a new boy came down from New York City and Mr. Raeburn said I could have him. I fell in love with the lad's beautiful blue eyes as soon as he walked into the library, and he regarded me with equal fervor, but it took only two nights in date hall to realize that his fervor was demented. This sad wretch, my first love, died mysteriously in a ditch the next summer. I would have felt responsible because I rejected him, except for the fact that time transferred his love to a professor's daughter.

Most any student was welcome at our innovative college. No credentials being necessary, we had some who could neither read nor write. No one ever flunked out, but there was one nice young man who could never earn a passing grade. Mr. Raeburn comforted him.

"There now, son, we'll just tear up that old report card. You just keep trying. We need you around here."

All the professors were interesting, and interested in me, but my disillusion about their wisdom set in early. The old lady who taught biology had one passionate aim in life,—to refute the heresy of evolution. Each new student from the sinful North increased her anxiety that evil doctrine might creep into her stronghold of pure fundamentalism. She required that each of us submit a weekly paper on a biology subject, and the Ohio smart-alecks invariably chose some forbidden subject. It was her custom to address us formally.

"Miss Crawford, what is your topic?"

"Hybrid seed corn."

Immediately I ceased to exist for the day.

"Mr. Sensibaugh, what is the subject of your paper?"

"Evolutionary changes in the pack rat."

And Hugh dematerialized also.

"Miss Saunders, what is your topic?"

"Mountain laurel."

"Very well, Miss Saunders, you may read your paper."

Then the tense angry lines in the face of the old fighter relaxed.

Another fine religious lady taught us both history and German, but she admitted frankly that she knew very little German. Since I had a mother from Stuttgart, the professor assumed I was an authority and proudly gave me an A plus. (Knowing little more than Danke Schoen and Du bist ein Dummkopf, I didn't fool the professor the next year at Miami, and barely got D.) For history class, a little more was required of us students. Namely, a wide-eyed horrified appreciation of the professor's salacious tales of the sexual orgies of the medieval popes. Grinning in delight, she regaled us with tales, including a description of a party held in the papal grape arbor in which naked women crawled around on all fours. Not much concerned with other aspects of history, she had time to tell us about her foster daughter, a hopeless child whose nose was half eaten away by some mysterious ailment. Sometimes the little girl came along to class, and the professor would instruct her, "Tell the class how nice it was of Mamma to take you out of the poor house."

My favorite professor was a droll, Lincolnesque type who taught and enjoyed the Bible. Although his contract must have called for pounding home God's literal dictation of the Bible, he generally soft pedalled the propaganda. In his class we responded to roll call with a Biblical verse, and this became great sport.

"Maxey."

"Turn away your eyes from me for they disturb me."

"Hughie."

"Stolen water is sweet and bread eaten in secret is pleasant."

"Elsie."

"A little sleep, a little slumber, and poverty will come upon you like a vagabond."

"Piney."

"Come let us take our fill of love until morning."

He never criticized our selections, so long as they were accurate, but his eyes twinkled in his carefully sobered face. He disappointed me at first by never answering my questions, but only turning them aside with a mild joke; so I gave up queries, being too busy anyway searching through the Bible. My nutty New York friend, I was told, stood up in another section of the religion course and asked for advice on what to do if you were so much in love you didn't want to live. The professor Ann-Landered with a straight-face "Try eating a mess of fishhooks."

He also taught Homiletics, which I understood to be the art of expounding endlessly on a verse of scripture, and he was partly in charge of the preacher boys, the battalion of young men who went out into the country churches for hundreds of miles to spread the gospel. On Monday mornings the boys reported their victories, and at the end of the summer's evangelistic treks, they charted their scores on the blackboard for everyone's admiration. Our classroom was decorated with the jubilant announcement that Orby came out ahead by saving one hundred and thirteen souls at Wildcat Ridge, while Edsel breathed down his neck with one hundred ten scalps from his revival at Chinkapin Hollow. I have forgotten how they counted the re-conversions and the re-res, but probably it was two for one.

Whatever sophisticated expectations I might have had about social life faded into the bucolic pleasure of apple peelings when some kind citizen donated a barrel of fruit. In our rigidly constricted lives, any opportunity to mingle with males brought on girlish high blood pressure. My table assignment offered me a natural role as mother to seven younger students. At the other end of the table was Maxey, tallest boy in the school. Our littlest at dinner was Emory, Maxey's age but half his size, and our youngest was Tossy, all of fourteen. There was no high school in her hollow, and she sped through eight years of schooling in four; so then, to pass the time until some college would accept her, she took the eight years over again. Maxey and I enjoyed pretending that we would spend the rest of our lives together, and we planned to name our eighth and ninth children Lamentations and Ecclesiastes.

We were all such sincere and pious students that usually the worst infraction of the rules was to pass notes. We could transmit them under the table right beneath the president's eyes from shoe to shoe, each operator of the underground telegraph reaching down casually to pick up a handkerchief or scratch a bite. There was one clear Saturday afternoon, however, when the Devil had his way with us. A professor agreed to lead a hike. He seldom looked back; so the boys and girls paired off and someone must have been left out, for it was reported right afterwards to the president that couples had been HOLDING HANDS! What shame and disgrace! Mr. Raeburn gave us a lecture that night that brought tears to our eyes. Piney, on probation anyway because she had added red food coloring to the rinse water for her hair, was asked to leave. Mr. Raeburn said that only because of his merciful heart was he keeping the school open at all. At Caney Creek College, a fine example of what he wanted our school to be, a hundred students had been expelled recently for courting. If we were ready to hold hands, we could get married, and he was building a row of cabins for married student housing.

By the beginning of June six couples had taken up residence, my roommate Virgie becoming one of the brides. So far as I have heard, she and her preacher boy are still glad they found each other.

I suppose none of us at the school were above a little trickery. On our work assignments we learned how to work a little extra for ourselves. The furnace firing boys enticed the hens to lay in a nearby barrel; then the coal shovel held into the flames became a fair egg fryer. I found that the best task was breakfast duty, even though it meant getting up at five-thirty to build a fire in the old cook stove. Coal heaped outdoors in the rain and snow was a little hard to manage without a shovel, but we usually had the fire roaring by the time we'd picked the roaches out of the bread dough. A vat of cornmeal mush or a few hundred biscuits with a panful of lard and flour gravy was a fairly good breakfast for the mob. It was a shame there wasn't enough milk for the coffee and mush of that crowd, but we felt at least the breakfast crew should be well nourished.

Virgie and I moved with three other girls into the attic above the dean's house. Somebody's mother sent us an electric burner; so we saved our pennies to buy cocoa, sugar, and canned milk for the comfort of bedtime refreshments. Then one day we were lectured in chapel about the sin of selfishness, and the conscience stricken Virgie confessed about our stove and turned it in. Mr. Raeburn made another speech then all about how it was not in our best interests to eat between meals because we had such a good balanced diet. We believed him, weeping into our beans, because there was something about that man's talking that could make you feel guilty about stroking your chin. It was a funny thing about that diet. For the only time in my life I became underweight.

Although I did not fit into this school religiously, I really loved the crazy place, perhaps because all of us had fun being poor together.

One day Maxey did not appear for supper, and Emory sneaked me a package which contained Maxey's only pair of pants. He'd been trying to press a crease in them so that he would look sharp for Date Hall and he'd burned a flat iron shaped hole clear through one leg. I borrowed a piece of material from the president's wife, who promised to keep my secret that I was doing such an unmaidenly thing as to handle a boy's trousers, and I patched them the best I could. Maxey wore them the rest of the year. There was no nonsense there about being well dressed, since being dressed at all was the general aim.

All along I knew that this college academically was a poor grade elementary school, and when I learned that attending Miami University would cost no more, I washed dishes in a summer camp for another hundred dollar nest egg and went to a real college. I didn't have much fun there. Since then I've attended and taught in other colleges, and I have met some great people, but I have to admit that noble spirit, generosity and courage are not universal. In fact, I have come up against some pretty sneaky varmints in learned circles.

At Miami I graded English themes for a professor who listed at the start what grades I should put on the papers for the entire year, based on the student's entrance exam scores. She said that if anyone complained I should be careful to mark every single tiny error so that there could be no further flak. She never bothered reading a theme herself.

And there was the Eugenics prof who required that we find a family suitable for a "scientific" proof that degeneracy is inherited. That was when I wrote my first successful work of fiction.

Often I met indifference to students' troubles like that stunning experience at Hiram, and sometimes it was directed at me. A prissy Miami expert advised me, instead of getting an additional job, to go home pacified by the knowledge that briefly I had been a "college woman," since by her calculations I was already putting in thirty hours a day on jobs and school. I didn't bother to explain that I could cook dinner, study Sociology, and watch somebody's baby all at the same time.

As a graduate student in the University of Chicago I was pleased to meet a resourceful dean, but only after I became hysterical about the same old advice that I give up and go home.

"If I'd listened to that kind of nonsense I'd still be pulling weeds in an onion patch," I blubbered.

The austere dean mobilized her forces, scurried out of the office and returned with that grand old lady of social work, Sophonisba Breckinridge, who hired me on the spot to index her latest book. She brushed away my gratitude. It was strictly business.

More than twenty years later, tired of listening while clients told me how they hated their fathers, mothers, husbands, wives, and new born babies, I was about to earn a Master's Degree in sociology and begin teaching. I worked out a resume that I thought sounded intriguing, on the first printed batch making the Freudian slip of listing the year of my graduate degree as the year of my birth. My daughter Connie helped me go through Lovejoy's handbook on American colleges, judging from the printed blurb about each one how religious they were (for purposes of avoidance), and we sent out letters in floods like the Christmas cards of a new liquor store. I can't remember how in the world we financed the postage. For a month afterwards we watched the mailman stagger to our box, weighted down with the "Sorry" replies.

After another decade as a social worker, though, the pretensions of that field began to seem even more galling. Since the flight from affluence to my new location in a Western town, I am again involved with a college. I absolutely know that in this college there is more open-hearted honesty than meanness, and I have found more broad minds than narrow ones. It isn't a religious place. If my disenchantment with academia seems to be all mixed up with my disappointing relationships with God and his minions, that is as it was. Disillusions about those who walk hand-in-hand with the deity have permeated my whole life, possibly because I never was selected for that onerous honor.

6

Religion hid its sneaky head in my life until I was fourteen. All of us had been Christened in the Lutheran faith, but after we moved down to the woods, we had no transportation to church and we grew up spiritually ignorant. My mother felt guilty and sad about that, but she firmly believed that holy instruction should be left to the Lutheran minister, and he never found his way to our muddy road. Accordingly, religious ideas made me as mysteriously uncomfortable as other secret subjects. I turned crimson over all such words as God, unwell, Jesus, family way, heaven, breast, bosom and dear. In English class when it came time for me to recite, I would count the lines ahead to estimate when my turn would come, and if there were any awful words in the text, I would need to develop a coughing fit or a blinding headache. I could no more have said bosom outloud than I could have sworn at the teacher.

The gospel finally came our way in the shape of Georgie Porgie, the butcher boy, as we called the bumbling young fellow who drove the grocery truck on its weekly hinterland tour. One Saturday after he had written up my mother's order of flour, lard, sugar, salt pork, Fels

Naptha soap and three-pound-for-a-quarter hamburger, Georgie made a little speech.

"Our church is having a contest with the Painesville outfit to see who can have the best attendance for the next month, and I want to invite you and your kids to come. It's real nice to set down together on Sunday to study the so-called Bible and have a little prayer session and so on; so how about coming to Sunday School and church this week and see how it sets with you?"

My mother was thrown into a confusion of distress and pleasure. Despite her obligation to save us for the true faith, she was proud that anybody would invite us to go anywhere.

"My goodness, that's awful nice of you folks, I must say, but I just don't know. They ain't got anything nice enough to wear to church. The girls don't have hats."

Georgie blew away her objections. "They go to school, don't they? Whatever they wear to school is good enough. We ain't a bit fancy, and hardly any of the women folks wear hats."

My mother's nervous hands readjusted her side combs to catch her straggling fine hair. "But it's just that we're a little short right now, and I just don't see how they could go."

No one knew better than Georgie how short we were. For many weeks he'd had nothing but promises to take back to his father's cash register, but Sunday competition meant more than money right then. "We're not out for the money. Course I'd be the last one to deny that it comes in handy, ha-ha, but we like folks to come if they got nothing but buttons for the collection plate. You come along now on Sunday."

It was unthinkable that my mother should consider going, with all her social handicaps, but she sat up all night to make her children decently clothed for their initial expedition. Not eager to take up the invitation, since my school friends ridiculed all churches and I had some notion that my free time was too valuable, I couldn't back out when I saw the pretty cream colored dress with embroidered pockets my mother had fashioned from a heavy curtain. Once we were thrown into the new world of sentence prayers, church suppers with their bottomless cartons of ice cream, and youth Hallowe'en parties, church did chew up a large part of the week. But we always went if the car would start. We four kids and the congregation benefitted mutually. The benign believers who attended there showed us that the Crawford children were as good as anyone else and superior to some, since we asked so many questions that everybody else had to go home and study for the next week. When I was seventeen they appointed me Sunday School superintendent, and then proceeded to knead the lumps out of our resistance to joining a non-Lutheran church. That was the terrible step that our mother trusted Gott-im-Himmel to save us from, but we couldn't hold out against the kindness and admiration.

There was one dear soul so sensitive to our poverty that she invariably slipped me a handkerchief when the minister went into some high geared conversation with the Almighty, because she knew that my nose always dripped if my head hung down. When she backed me up against the thorns of disbelief with a sweet "But you do love Jesus, don't you?" what could I say?

Sure, I'd always had a sneaking love for Jesus, but I didn't want to say so. As they say about sex, it's easier to go ahead than to talk about it. We found ourselves committed, and the time came when we had to face our mother. Marge, usually so meek and agreeable, led the fight for us, staunchly holding out despite our mother's white-faced hysteria.

"How can you say you want to join the church? You are already church members, ever since you were Christened when you were little babies. It's confirmation they have at your age, not more baptism. You're going against your own church. Pa! Tell them they can't do it. It's all your fault anyway that they never got to the Lutheran church. You can hitch up the horse fast enough when you want to go bumming."

My father goggled over the top of his Argosy magazine. "They're your kids, woman. One church is the same as another anyway. All they want is a poor man's money."

We went ahead with our plans, experiencing first hand the misery of being persecuted for Christ's sake; it didn't feel blessed at all with our mother not communicating except for her tears falling into the dishwater. The new crop of male converts was baptized one Sunday and the females the next, so that the water could be chastely replaced during the week. Ben was too young for the ceremony; so Milton took his vows first. We all hoped and expected that "going forward" would improve Milton's irritating personality, and we were not disappointed. He emerged from the tank so quiet, serene and withdrawn that my mother began to cheer up, thinking that perhaps her first born would become a clergyman after all, which would be a credit to her no matter if he did make a mistake in the denomination.

On our sacremental day Margaret and I carried a sack of clean clothes, as we set out with our monkish brother for the hallowed event. Feeling mostly silly as we stepped into today's version of the river Jordan, we clutched our noses when the minister in his fisherman waders dumped us over backwards so that we could be thoroughly immersed. Then we dripped up the steps and off stage where we shivered into dry clothes while the congregation gave thanks that two more bad eggs were safely recycled.

Margaret and I exchanged abashed glances, wordlessly expressing uneasiness about how we were going to manage concealing our disenchantment. Milton solemnly handed us into the Overland roadster he'd bought for fifteen dollars at a foreclosure sale, and drove slowly homeward as befitted a car load of new saints.

"Do you notice how different the world looks?" Milton inquired reverently.

We peered around at the dusty sumac as we clattered over the same bumpy New York Central tracks we'd crossed that morning before we'd been saved.

Marge took over. "Yeah, yeah, I guess it does look kinda different."

"You do feel like a new person, don't you?" Milt seemed anxious. "You've been born again."

Marge and I became very busy adjusting towels around our wet heads while we sneaked guilty looks at each other. Suddenly Milt hooted with sacreligious laughter.

"All you got was wet!" he shouted. Temporarily unhinged by the unqualified success of his week-long masquerade, Milt had to stop driving while he beat his feet against the floorboards in gleeful spasms. We laughed too. It was a great thing, baptism, uniting the three of us in unbelief, but we felt sick about the trouble we'd started at home. We didn't talk much at the dinner table that day and we were very quick to jump up when the milk pitcher needed refilling. No one had to ask us to wash dishes afterwards.

Despite my growing agnosticism, I stuck with our unfashionable band of believers through high school, substituting Christian Endeavor rallies for the dances and movies my friends attended. My church taught that dancing was evil, well, not exactly that, but better left alone because it led to evil on the back seats of touring cars on the way home. I wished I could think so too, but my feet ached for the waltz and fox-trot that I knew I was too clumsy to learn. Religion could be exciting also, what with the leadership of meetings, speech making, and teaching Sunday School. Sometimes there were disastrous consequences. One young lady became an embittered atheist after a spell as my student, and she has held her fall from innocence against me ever since.

The Kentucky institution which I attended for my first year of college was part of our sect, but more rigorously anti-intellectual and evangelistic. It was the Sunday afternoon custom for a group of Bible-bearing students to flood the country people with gospel and song, and I was once coerced into going. I thought that I wouldn't disgrace myself carrying alto in Blest Be The Tie That Binds, but I knew that I'd die on the spot if anyone suggested that I lead the prayers. I needn't have worried. Those semiliterate hill folk were most enthusiastic hymn singers, Bible readers, and beseechers for inner peace and outward prosperity, that they weren't taking a back seat for any college kids, no matter how high faluting. Even so I felt uncomfortably haloed, and the afternoon sent me a little farther along the trail that led away from old fashioned religion.

There's nothing quite so effective to turn believers into doubters and doubters into agnostics and atheists as a good old-fashioned fundamentalist college. During my Freshman year in Kentucky, religion surrounded me like hot and steamy marsh quicksand, but I was becoming more and more sturdy in my convictions and made steady progress toward truth and light except for one major set-back. At the time of my two week romance, we were all expected to attend Sunday night revival meetings. During one come-on hymn, even while I was vowing that nobody was going to have any effect on me whatever, I saw my sweet but stupid Henry ambling up the aisle to accept Jesus, and suddenly with a will of their own, my feet were carrying me up to the altar after him. In the years that followed I have followed other men, some of whom didn't know any more than Henry did, to some kind of promise of bliss, but even way back there when I was a dewey eyed nineteen, I knew my pilgrimage had more to do with chemistry than with religion. Yet in the Kentucky sense, I was saved that night. I was such a queer kind of convert, with skeptical comments falling faster than ever from my reckless mouth, that my religious friends became sadly confused. They told me earnestly that they were asking God to help me with my problem when they met for Wednesday night prayer. I had to bear the humiliation of having my private soul discussed in public, and contemplated with horror the possibility that their prayers might be answered. However, so far as I ever heard, their communications were one way.

It took a disgusting episode in a little church near Miami University to drive me completely away from fundamentalist religion.

One Sunday night in Christian Endeavor I tried to set the embryonic student preacher right by some pointed questions about his theology. Among those gathered together in the name of mindless faith was a ratty female with a retinue of runny-nosed, whimpering kids who should have been home in bed. Holding her soggy baby with the festering sores around its gaping mouth, this woman took it upon herself to save me from damnation.

"I used to be just like you." She wound up her argument with a friendly smile that revealed blackened shards of teeth in swollen gums. "Yes, I was just like you, always asking questions, doubting the good Lord's word, trying to prove something." The baby in her arms whimpered louder. Opening the clasp of her filthy handbag, the mother rooted around in a peck of refuse for a pacifier which she then lubricated with her own rabid spit before poking it into the child's mouth. "I was just like you. But with the help of prayer, I got over all that."

I skedaddled fast and didn't stop running from religion for a dozen years. About that time, my little girls began associating with Baptists and came home mouthing absurdities about being washed in blood; so I joined the most liberal church in town. Happily discovering that when a doctrinal heirloom is set to music, the sickening quality is somewhat neutralized, I joined the choir too. The girls sang in children's choirs, became candlelighters and church camp attenders. All of us looked forward to the double Easter morning program when everyone in the packed church looked beautiful and the Ladies' Aid served breakfast to the choirs between services.

There was a point along there when I could no longer swallow the communion grape juice, feeling certain that I would choke on cannibalistic practices, no matter how vestigial. No one ever questioned why I began passing on the trays without partaking, but I felt that the shocked eyes of the whole choir were upon me each time. When we moved to Cleveland after Meredith was fourteen, she discovered the Unitarian church and led us there. Since then I've always been quick to admit that churches have something to offer, especially the Unitarian, because that was where I learned to dance and I've never been sorry about that.

People are still praying about me, though. Even today, the dearest young man and woman I know in my present community, have confided that they think perhaps their mission in life is to bring me into the fold. They say that they like me,—no, it's stronger than that, they say they love me as I am, and I believe them. What change they hope to see in me if I should be able to glibly recite the Christian formula some day, I can't imagine, but I forgive them their fervor. After all, I'm not too proud to admit that some of my best friends are Christians.

I've also had some first rate positive shocks about religious people. Once upon a time I was prejudiced against Catholics, believing they were all so wobbly in their logical upper story that one good argument would send them crashing the gates of the nearest mental hospital, that they never did any thinking but only rearranged lines of the catechism, and that all they needed for happiness was mass on Sunday and a piece of fish on Friday. That was before I met Father Ross and the sisters Evelyn, Shirley, and Gail.

I was trying to get rich in my spare time with a real estate license, and my hottest client was Father Ross, who needed a large house where he could strengthen the morale of ex-alcoholics with community life and understanding. Our real estate agency had no suitable place; so I called another agent who directed us to just the right address. He said he'd lost the key, but we could climb through the second floor back window which he'd left open, if we'd walk up the back stairs. Father Ross and I met in front of the old mansion in a howling thunderstorm, and found our way around the block and through the littered alley to the back yard. After treading gently among the broken whiskey bottles and rusty fenders, we guessed that the neighbor kids must have hacked off every other step to the high porch for wiener roast fires. Both of us being tall, we didn't mind too much taking giant steps until a trembling eave trough overhead gave up the ghost, drenching us with a cascade of icy water and rotten leaves. We kept climbing, such stalwart souls we were, commenting that the place ought to be cheap enough. As we crawled through the window, open all right since some vandal had bashed in the glass, Father Ross said that he didn't know any other woman mad enough to enter such a dump except the Dominican sisters who had just come to town. He thought I should meet them. Inside the house we gazed awe-struck at what we thought was a huge sky-light until we saw more clearly that a piece of the roof sized like a queenly bed had descended, and a flock of pigeons were swooping in to get out of the rain.

I never got a cut of Father Ross' down payment fund, since the funding for his project did not come through, but I struck gold with his suggestion that I meet the sisters. Fresh from the over-protective cloister, they had come to that wicked and dangerous city of Washington to help in any way possible. They cut off their habits, and waded into the fetid community problems, helping in schools and clinics and welfare offices. In their time off, they wanted to see the world. You've never really heard the Marine band play or eaten Georgetown's crepes Suzettes or gathered with friends around the dinner table unless you've shared the excitement with someone like those eager girls who hadn't even been inside a private home for fifteen years. Evelyn and Shirley stayed with us one summer, and they were such fun that other fascinating people began dropping in, sometimes for breakfast, when they heard that there might be a leftover piece of Sister Evelyn's apple pie. Jokes rolled along from day to day, some of them clear across the country to the Mother houses.

One that is still rolling is what we called "The Night of the Rape."

Our household consisted at the time of the two nuns, my daughter Meredith and me, and our unsociable brown-skinned roomer Clarence, who said he was so sick of men after twenty years of military service that he wanted to live somewhere within the sound of women's voices. But he didn't want to get involved. Keeping aloof, he was still drawn to the merriment of Meredith and the sisters, becoming very close to being fond of them. One night when Clarence knew that I was expecting to be out of town, he heard stealthy footsteps on the stairs and along the hall toward my room. He didn't think it sounded like me but he wasn't sure. After a few explosive silent moments, Clarence saw by the glimmer of the alley light through his window that his door was noiselessly opening. He switched on his bedside light and there, creeping on hands and knees toward him, was menacing evil personified. One glimpse was all he got before the creature sprang erect and dashed down the stairs. The front door slammed. Half paralyzed with fear that the intruder might have only pretended to leave,

Clarence sprang into action with the thought that the nuns and Meredith might be murdered in their beds downstairs. Shouting their names, he burst without knocking into their rooms. Never in their adult lives had the sisters been seen in bed by a man.

Shirley went to pieces, shrieking, "I don't want to die a virgin martyr."

The more composed Evelyn pulled them both together, and everyone thought they'd better have some scrambled eggs and toast with plenty of coffee prepared for the police who were soon swarming over the house.

I'm a little sorry I missed the fun, although I might not be alive to tell the story if I had been there. They told me afterwards that the young detective was so confused to find such a strange assortment of citizens under one roof that he kept tearing pages out of his notebook to start over fresh. As he eyed the bathrobed sisters he was just repeating doubtfully, "Now you say you are Dominican sisters?" when the front door opened and a girl dressed in bright orange walked in with a cheery smile and apparently no need for introductions. She knew nothing of the early morning break-in, but showed no surprise that her chosen sisters were serving coffee to half a dozen policemen and a nervous brown man who'd forgotten to put in his teeth.

"Don't bother getting up," she said. "I can't stay because I'm on my way to mass. I just wanted to let you know that we decided we wouldn't wear our veils this afternoon when we go to see Rosemary's Baby. We thought it might not look right."

The detective laid his pen carefully on the table and started to tear out another sheet.

"Never mind that," Sister Evelyn explained. "You won't need information about Sister Gail. She doesn't live here. Yes, she really is a nun too, but Sister is experimenting with colors."

Let me make it quite clear that none of those dear sisters ever tried to convert me. Instead of evangelistic ranting, they gave me respect and appreciation for my own beliefs. You can't do much more than that.

There is one other lady of the faith who brought me an unexpected blessing. In my late forties when I was a low-paid social worker with two children to support, I began dreaming of graduate school. A Master's Degree would surely put cleats on my mountain climbing boots, so that I could escape from poverty valley. Besides, I was sick of social workers who explained in so many dull words why they weren't about to do what their agencies were chartered for. In graduate school there would be clear sighted intelligent people with long range vision. It was the same old dream in another form, and I still had no money. By that time I was pretty leary about asking for help. Years before, when the little sum of twenty-five dollars would have saved me from disaster, I wrote to a former employer who had assured me that I had only to request aid, and she would send it. Her reply to my pleas was a chilly, unconditional "NO."

But there was this unassuming philanthropist I knew slightly. For three years I tried to lasso the necessary courage to talk with her, but couldn't do it. Finally I outlined my ambitious plans to her in a letter, asking if she would help. Then I sank into a depression, pulling over myself the mill-stone conviction that the mail would bring rejection or perhaps no word at all.

Instead there came an early morning call, and I heard the voice of this dear lady saying, "I'll be happy to help you. I'm putting a check for a thousand dollars in the mail today. Please let me know when you need more."

I walked the floor, my cheeks wet with tears. It was like a handclasp with purest goodness, an overwhelming experience of graciousness. Even today, nearly ten years later, I still had many payments to go, and this angel urged me to wait until my second daughter was through college before sending the rest. Even today her letters are gems of encouragement and faith.

MEN

7

Perhaps I've always been a little confused about reality when it comes to men, and for that I vehemently
blame the printed page. Somewhere I'm sure I read in
black and white that when a man kissed you, it meant
he loved you. I know that all the novels taught that
destiny in the shape of an ever-loving husband waited on
some bus or elevator or plane or library alcove. All I had
to do was recognize him, and that wouldn't be any problem because he would be looking too, and lightning
would flash between our eyes.

It never worked out that way.

As I recall the interactional farces which fate staged
for me with some of the momentous men in my life, the
world goes all misty like an arty movie screen, and a
picture emerges of a ghostly city bus pulling up to the
corner of Thirteenth and Massachusetts, Southeast, in
Washington. I hear a voice intoning, "Make room, make
room. Please step to the rear," while a crowd of men I
have loved, plus a few who loved me, all jostle aboard
together. What a fey gang!

There is Henry, the fellow from the Kentucky college,
the one with the fanatic blue eyes. Next, comes Otto. I

would know that leather jacket anywhere, and can almost smell it. The one with the sideburns is Elgin. And that tall one, that angular temple to suffering, is Duane to whom I was married for ten interminable years.

Otto was a countryman, the kind of fellow so common back in the late twenties. He raised roses, worked at the Rubber Works, and bounced around the rutted side roads in his new four hundred dollar roadster. With that car he was always somebody's beau, not mine, for when we first met, I was fifteen to his twenty-nine. But he still sent the blood sugar coursing through my veins. He came to our house to talk horses with my father and argue religion with my brother. I fished hard for his attention, laughing hard at his jokes, sloshing water over his arctics as I trudged past with a brimming bucket, but it was no use. Once when I heard him say he didn't believe in Jesus, I tried the cold shoulder approach, drawing away in what I hoped was mature dignity to say, "I cannot consider any man my friend unless he believes in Jesus."

Otto thought that was uproarious. So did my brother; I stumbled red-faced up the dark stairway, always booby-trapped with junk, and denied the men my company for an evening. That bothered them not at all.

Five years later, however, when I was home from college for Christmas vacation, I had fallen into a doze in the downstairs bedroom and heard my mother telling someone that I was a pretty sick girl. They said Otto took the news like a stab in the heart, and sat all night by the bed wringing cold cloths to drape over my fever-ish face. When I recovered, I had a devoted swain, but the way that particular script was written, no one fell into anyone's arms. I went back to school in Kentucky, after a date to a comic movie in which none of the jokes were funny, and holding hands in the cramped movie seats gave me a pain in the elbow.

A few months later Otto went berserk. Following improvement at the State Hospital, he came home for a peaceful week-end, but then without warning or histrionics he wandered out to the yard, doused himself with gasoline and struck a match. I read the news in a letter from home in the same kind of befuddled daze that I had witnessed his outpouring of love, unable to believe that I had caused either phenomenon.

But I could never really be sure!

It was the next summer Henry died. It did nothing for my self image to know that the only men who thought they cared about me were both of unsound mind. Could a commoner be cursed by an evil fairy? Would all the men in my life be part of the same kind of nightmare?

Duane is dead too, by his own decision in the last act of a life-long drama in which he tried to control the emotions of his family. Duane was always in pain. Overwork wracked his muscles, arthritis crippled his joints. The perfidy of the dear ones for whom he worked night and day, as well as the sinfulness of the world, tormented his soul. No one lived according to his ideas of proper conduct, but we did live in fear of his moods. And I didn't even know he was moody before we were married! I saw him as a kindly contented man who loved children and wanted a snug home. He was much older.

"But age doesn't matter," I said, "if two people have the same life style and ideas."

Whatever merit my philosophizing might have had, I guess I didn't give enough respect to the little word *if.*

He thought he was getting an old fashioned hausfrau, an adoring Griselda. I thought at the very least I was getting a paternal lap for my little Meredith whose father Elgin had long since departed into the never-never land of new love. Three days after our wedding, Duane stopped speaking to me, maintaining a morose silence while I pleaded that he tell me what was wrong. I can see now that I should have called him a great joker and swooned with laughter when he explained that he was offended because I had waved at a friend driving a taxi. No decent married woman would wave to a man, he said. I took it all seriously, trying to adjust to please him until I could convert him to greater trust and liberality, which shouldn't be impossible since I was a caseworker and knew how much talking helps.

The next week he began looking at Meredith with cold hostility. "If there's anything I can't abide, it's a great big four year old wanting to sit on her mother's lap. Go outside and play. Your mother's tired."

As a working mother, I had little chance to see my daughter all day, but I didn't dare express my outraged feelings. If he wasn't angry already, he might become so, and if he was already in a temper, it could get worse. Like the stupid ninny my brother always called me, I tried to live with the situation, comforting my child when her step-father wasn't looking.

A man of generally wintry attitudes with unexpectedly sunny spells, he hated nearly everyone except small babies. Little things too young to question his authority, they could do no wrong, but as soon as they began asking for reasons, his love cooled. One day he brought home three delicate hemlock seedlings he'd found in the woods, and I thought what perfect children they would be for him. Tiny, immobile, pliant.

When Duane woke up to the knowledge that for some inexplicable reason I liked many people, he felt he'd been cheated or soon would be. Yet this aching misanthrope could go all out for Christmas, with gifts even for those he hated, and when confined in a psychiatric hospital where he was treated tenderly, he blossomed briefly into good health.

I can easily hear Otto and Duane and Henry talking over old times as my fantasied bus approaches Despondency Flats. I expect Otto would initiate communication.

Otto: "Hello, Buddy. Going along, are you? Can't get my head clear lately, but this is the bus to Erie, isn't it?"
Henry: "Erie."
Otto: "You were there, where I was; where the sky went black and blight hit the flowers."
Henry: "Roses, roses, my heart's a bleeding rose. All my life bleeding, crying, hurting all along Seventh and Third but nobody sees. Come to me and I will give you something. Something for nothing, nothing is me."
Otto: "Hey, you don't want to talk that way. We're on the right road now."
Duane: "Getting nowhere. World's gone mad. Evil, evil, sin. Folks used to help each other but you can't find anyone to help any more. No use anyway. Everybody's no damn good, specially women."
Henry: "Women. That's what I forgot. Girl, mamma, lady. Go way. You big boy now. Light in the attic, don't go out. See me. I hurt. Somebody listen."
Duane: "Shut off my light and heat, they did. Always somewhere, church and meetings eight nights a week, in hotels even. No worth-while women left since Mother passed. No use. No use. Can't go on."
Otto: "There's lights ahead, closer and closer."
Henry: "All lighty, like Macy's."
Duane: "It's Ma! Ma! Going to milk old Brindle. Swinging her lantern!"

Meanwhile in the back of the bus is a garrulous crowd, all in some branch of the people-helping industry. Tony is that lanky psychiatrist, and the chubby huggable fellow in the clerical collar is Jimmy. I met them in group psychotherapy with Fritz Perls poking holes in our defenses, all of us noting expansively how much more lovable everyone was getting. But they really weren't always such dears.

I believed Tony was God's gift to the neurotic world, until that day when he said, "You're getting the wrong idea about our relationship. I'm a happily married man, and even if I weren't married, I'd never consider you because of the class difference."

Jimmy told me by telephone. "I decided I'd better tell you before we go any farther. I'm sorry I got into this, because I already have a stable full of women and there's no need to add another to the string."

Beasts, both of them. Yet when I ran into Tony at a national conference years later, his smile was genuinely affectionate. Later I went through a serious illness, weakness and worry sapping my will to live, until Jimmy brought me flowers and held my hand. Then I could take up my bed and walk again.

Two men named Fred have struck up a conversation in my persisting fantasy. They should. Although they never met, each one reigned in my love life, mostly in imagination, for many years. Fred B. and I carried grave responsibilities together as we wrestled with lifetime decisions for others. Should we recommend that the judge remove Josie from her parents' custody forever? Could we somehow scrounge a home for buck-toothed Merton or allow him to be condemned to the boys' industrial school? Could we afford to interfere with Mrs. Yam's choking domination of her family of boys unless we had something better to offer?

Our interdependence was tender but very, very chaste, although one canny paranoid client claimed that we committed eye intercourse. Fred suffered from a peculiar, noncommunicable illness, and when he recovered, I mysteriously acquired the same problem. He quit his job over injustices, and so did I.

"We'll always be together really," he told me. "Wherever I go, I'll see that there will be a place for you too. I'll always love you. Nothing can ever change that."

My feeling for him was so encompassing, so overwhelming that I couldn't use the word love at all, but what I said meant much the same thing.

It was all bunk, applesauce, piffle!

After years of moving around the country in different directions, Fred B. and I happened to settle in Washington on jobs within ten minutes of each other. I saw him about five years ago for lunch, but since then one thing and another have interfered with renewing our association. The fact is that Fred didn't get around to writing much, and neither did I. My daughter saw him in the government cafeteria once, and he told her that our love for each other is the kind that never changes no matter how many years go by. Well, maybe. People like to talk like that. I suspect it makes them feel faithful and constant, but my calculations indicate three hundred and sixty days to be the average life span of love unless it's handy, without parking problems or home-life hassle.

A waning love is like radio music so beautiful you can't bear to turn it off when you go out; so the melody fades as you walk to the elevator, and all the way through traffic you feel better because you know it still sounds through the air. Sometimes you think you can hear it, but you don't really. It's the same as seeing the beloved's face in the clouds after staring at his photograph.

Fred Jay came into my life when I was a working student in the University of Chicago library. I saw this young but mature looking baldpate tilt his chair against the wall and study a page intently, but he would flash me a half smile when I came near with an armful of books to shelve. He walked home with me one night to my basement cubby hole for a cup of tea, and I can remember telling him the whole story of my life until he kissed me. Long afterwards when I could see that the intensity of my feeling in no way was matched by his, I asked him why he had kissed me that first night if he didn't love me.

"Got tired of hearing you talk," he said.

Nevertheless, I knew it was deathless devotion in my heart for him, and I had the good authority of hundreds of novels that love's golden purity sometimes went undiscovered by one of the partners for decades. I had the strength to wait and love.

In those days a student went to graduate school because he couldn't find a job, since most anyone could find some means of support on campus. Crippled by the Depression, Fred Jay never had found a real job, and now at twenty-seven, he was considered too old for flunky-type spots. Though somewhat eccentric in his life style, he was generous with his poverty. On his last few pennies, we shared a bowl of chili with two spoons, and he introduced me to Father Devine's Heaven where any starveling could have a meal with fifteen cents and "Peace." When Fred was locked out of his room for back rent, what could I do but share my powder blue attic with him, informing the landlady that my husband had come back to me. Fred carried the Tribune want-ads along to class, and checked out every measly ad, but was always turned away. I found an apartment to clean for a dollar a day and supper, and with the consolation that I was helping Fred as I choked down the rubber tube, I sold a pint of gastric juice for a ten spot. In the spring, we were both enfolded in the loving arms of the welfare administration to be what they called caseworkers, and the sky turned blue. I began to hear wedding bells.

It was no fantasy. They really were ringing.

One evening as I waited for the Wentworth Avenue street car, another caseworker blew to a stop beside me amid a swirl of dirty newspapers and chilly wind. She didn't know about my domestic arrangements.

"Guess what I just heard," she chortled. "Fred Jay and Marva are getting married next week!"

I said I hadn't heard and went directly home to tell the bridegroom in case he hadn't heard either. He miserably admitted his plans. "I should have told you, but I knew you'd hear it somewhere anyway."

He couldn't produce any valid reason for what I thought was contemptible behavior, or if he did, I couldn't grasp the significance. Next morning after he'd gone to work, I packed his belongings and set them outside the door. For days afterwards the pain was so real that I looked behind me on tenement stairways to see if I was leaving a trail of my heart's blood along the route of the dreary home visits. But heroines don't give up a man without a fight; so I called Marva and asked that she meet me in some South Parkway joint for a lunch discussion and she said it might be a good idea.

As we settled into a dark booth in a wooden silence, Marva filled her sails with a bracing wind. "I don't know why Fred is marrying me," she offered thoughtfully. "I think he really loves you, but I want him so much I'll take any chance."

There wasn't much to say after that. I didn't wish her any happiness but we parted without a fist fight. The newlyweds moved away, and I heard nothing for years except Fred's scrawl without return address on Christmas cards. I still loved him, his image helping me keep sane through all the bad times, through the loneliness of marriage and Duane's white rages and melancholy sloughs. After my husband's death, I boldly wrote the old alma mater for Fred's address, and then fate stepped in to send me five hundred miles to that very city for an adoption home study. So I went calling.

They entertained me by firelight in their woodsy cottage, Marva gracious, and Fred greeting me with the same kind of kiss that started the whole fifteen year fiasco. They'd had fantastic bad luck, illness bringing on worse money problems than mine, but they seemed unchanged. Their way of life showed that Fred had not lost his need for eccentricity. I could no longer see myself living with him. Suddenly I was able to give him up to Marva. We didn't sign any papers. Perhaps only I was aware of the difference in our relationship.

I've been there for dinner since, and once Fred drove me to the station.

"Marva says she invited you to come again," Fred's tone was suspicious. "Did she really?"

What was he up to? I said, "True, Fred, I've lost my zest for self-invites."

"Marva is a fool," he said tensely. "It isn't as if she doesn't know about us."

What was he trying to tell me? Nothing! Not one damn meaningful thing! Years ago a remark like that might have sent me into a six weeks' jitter of suppositions, but no more. His words issued automatically from the core of a sensitive man's personality, born of a feeble urge to live a little longer in a woman's dreams, probably for her sake. I need dreams, Fred knows, and it didn't cost him much. Like a sucker growing on a stump, all it needed was a few chemicals, a little sun, and a little leftover sap.

Back to the memory bus. How could I have looked twice at the pot and pan salesman from Indianapolis, or the Red Cross worker who stayed with us in Chicago when he flew in and found the hotels full? How much alike are the museum curator I met in Mexico City, and the English professor who tried so hard to help me appreciate Shakespeare. They are both so dainty, pallid and refined that they could be museum pieces themselves, and yet once I thought they were just right for me. I must have been most peculiar. If I need any further evidence that my seeing eye was a dog, let me point out Elgin. He hasn't noticed yet that there are no women passengers, and he settles posefully, looking around with eloquent brown eyes for someone to impress.

Elgin's mother wanted him to be a minister of the gospel. He tried hard, marrying an older woman who owned a hat shop. He claimed that she promised to pay his way through seminary if he'd make their situation legal, and then she threw him out with no more consideration than if he'd been a passe chapeau. He promptly married Joanna, a handicapped woman with a pension, who should have been grateful to have any husband. But her brothers interfered, especially after the birth of their son. Those brothers seemed to think Elgin should earn a living as well as being attentive and spiritually inclined. Perhaps it was just as well, Elgin said, although it was a shame about the little boy he left behind. He hadn't the money for an immediate divorce, but that hardly mattered.

"I realized that I don't really love Joanna, and I know that somewhere there is true love. I'm going to find it if it's the last thing I do."

He was so sweet and loving that I fancied myself the end of his search.

"You're so different," he said. "Before this, it was always married women I fell in love with. As a salesman I meet so many, and they are so hungry for love, particularly in the afternoon. Besides, I always think that if they should get pregnant, there's no harm done."

I could see that he tried to behave like a movie hero, but it never brought him lasting happiness. He described how once he told a three o'clock sweetheart that he loved her and she said, "Humph." Elgin was hurt. He knew he was mistaken again; so he silently pulled on his clothes and stole away to ring another doorbell.

We prevailed together until our baby girl was born, but on the zero night that he took us home from the hospital, Elgin explained that he'd been pretty magnanimous, staying around so long when his heart wasn't in it, but now he was about to leave. He'd always known that his true love wouldn't be like me at all, but a trim little brunette, and at last he'd found her, working at the foundry where he'd been hiding out from the draft board.

Reasoning that it was not what Elgin *was* but his potential that should concern me, I fought to keep this walking doll beside me, using my whole thimbleful of tricks. Tears, pleading, home baked bread, his little daughter in his arms, the pity of having to leave the baby to go back to work,—nothing moved him. So I tried evil.

Elgin and Brunetta worked the night shift, and one night as they waded around the snow drifts in the parking lot,—such a cute couple—they found me in my Terraplane blocking Elgin's Nash. Obviously shaken, Elgin asked what I wanted.

"I want you to come home."

Although violence was mostly confined to declared war in those days, Elgin hesitated, as if wondering if I might be armed. "I'll have to take Brunetta home first. She doesn't have a car. So you might as well go home and I'll be right along."

I said I'd make sure of that by following him.

The streets were too slippery for a wild chase. We were more like a funeral procession to Potter's Field as we wound through the midnight streets. Elgin actually asked if I'd like to have coffee with them when he reached her house but I declined, watching wearily as he escorted the girl tenderly to her door. Well, she wasn't exactly a girl since she had three growing children and a husband in the Marines, but anyway he saw her in before zooming off into the night like a tomcat with his back on fire. Halfway home, he parked the car beside the road and started walking. Guessing that he might be out of gas, I offered him a ride. He accepted with hanging head and cried all the way home!

I felt pretty cheap.

By this time, I knew that I didn't even like this unlucky Narcissus, but I thought our little girl needed her father, and I couldn't face up to failure. Fortunately Uncle Sam stepped in with a tap on the shoulder and broke up our unhappy home. Elgin responded manfully. He was enchanted with his new uniform and the chance to take Brunetta and her children along as far as the west coast. After a year he returned for a pleasant visit in which he took the baby for a walk in the park. I almost thought we were happily reunited, but when he said goodbye, he couldn't resist asking my congratulations on the fact that he and Brunetta were very happy together and would be getting married as soon as past legal adhesions could be dissolved. That was the last I heard of Elgin for fourteen years.

Little daughter Meredith grew up holding close the hope that someday she would see her own Daddy and he would compensate for the harshness of her stepfather. On the eve of her fifteenth birthday, a much forwarded letter bombed through our mail slot with an enclosed five dollar bill and a brief note. Meredith began an enraptured correspondence which revealed that Brunetta had long since departed with her three and their three, but Elgin was now cleaving unto wife number five.

There wasn't much else in his letters, which dwindled away until a package arrived for Meredith's graduation. She opened it hopefully, and there, life size, was the handsome face of Elgin himself. Slipping the picture out to see if there might be a letter or perhaps another bit of legal tender, Meredith learned that the gift was second hand. On the back were inked the words, "To Delores, with all my love, Elgin."

No longer illusion-laden, Meredith covered the winning smile with a magazine spread of sliced watermelon, but still she was mildly interested when he came through a few summers later and looked her up in the restaurant where she was waiting tables. With him was bride number six. They ate at her table, and the happy couple left the waitress a whole dollar tip.

I do hope no flavor of bitterness is creeping into this recital.

It is true that I no longer feel affection for Elgin, but I know that he never wanted to hurt anyone and that it takes one self-despising fool to want another. Many of my old loves still mean something very positive to me, and as a class, I love men very much. I have lived so long that I understand more about the cruel burdens and grinding conflicts to which they are subjected, and I can appreciate my good fortune in not having to share some of their troubles. If I think I have worries now, I sit back and picture what my life would be with Henry or Elgin around my neck, and all animosity toward men for so consistently letting me down fades away. Some failure to meet expectations is inevitable in man's wrestling match with society and its women. Like a rubber band, a man's strength can bear great strain in several directions at once, but then must shrivel and withdraw before meeting another crushing demand. Man's phallic behavior is dress rehearsal for his whole life.

Society says, "Here, Bub, trundle that cannon across the corn patch and kill off your cousins. What d'ye mean, you don't want to? You're a man, aincha?"

"Wade into that garbage, Buster, there's always another load on the way. Of course it's a dirty job. You a lilly or something?"

"Pick up that Conestoga, son, and carry it across the Missouri."

"Let's have a little action, guys, get that coupla million dollars worth of concrete up in the sky. You scared you didn't get the algebra right? Well, fix it somehow. We got a deadline to meet."

"Save the kid's life, doc, that's all I ask; you're supposed to be a doctor."

"Stick your legs under that desk, little fellow. Yeah, we know you want to run and play with those muscles you're so proud of, but you can forget that stuff. From now on you only need to be strong enough to carry your brain around. You work hard and we'll give you a nicer desk someday in a prettier cage."

"Give up your life work, Rex, the party has decided to run you for Congress. Stand up there and let them insult you. Yes, you just might lose everything, but this is for your country, man."

No matter how much prestige or education our lad acquires, when you look closely, he's obviously still Bub.

"Chart the course for those missiles, Dr. Kelley. A bunch of us fellows are planning to blow up the rest of the world. You think it isn't ethical? Look, Bub, we don't pay you for that kind of thinking."

And along the way, women get in their whacks.

"Love me, love me, love me. Be my constant hallucinogen. Be always strong, sexy, romantic and faithful. And incidentally, keep the bills paid and be nice to the kids."

It is astounding that any men survive to be fifty, incredible that some are still ambulatory at sixty, miraculous that a few continue year after year to be dependable, creative, loving, productive and sane. With what tremendous bursts of valor they carry on! God! How they try! Yet women will look around contemptuously and comment to each other:

"Look at that Edmund. No great shakes as a man, is he? The jerk makes a good meal ticket (or he's terrific with a paint brush, or he's fast at changing a tire, or he's great on skates, or crosswords, or in bed) but aside from that he's a washout."

With my grueling first hand experience proving that women have their burdens too, I sometimes get in that bitchy mood myself. Then I remember my father, a two hundred and fifty pound stripling with his nightshirt flapping around his bare legs as he challenged a neighbor's runaway mad bull one stormy night. That beast could easily have crushed my father against the barn door or tossed his mangled body into the haymow and both of them knew it, but my father had the invincibility of a tank that night as he battled the crazed bull because he knew it had to be done. That's a man for you.

There is one loved man in my life who is not aboard as the memory bus glides away from the curb. He travels alone in a kind of space capsule, intricately confined by the mechanisms of family, political, and professional considerations, but he keeps alert for those moments once a year or so when all the little tumblers of his locked safe fall into exactly the right places and he can splash down to be with me.

Once I might have attacked those locks with a sledge hammer.

HOUSES

8

On a summer morning in 1938 I debussed at sixty-third and Stoney Island in Chicago and found nothing open in that great roaring city; so I sat in Jackson Park slapping mosquitos and wondering down which murky street I would find my own little homeplace, a nook so cozy and comfortable that never again would I hesitate to be hospitable. Gone forever would be the prickling shame of visiting through a car window in the front yard because I couldn't bring myself to ask anyone to see our junky house. After paying a quarter's tuition in the graduate social work school, I could afford one week's rent, lay in a supply of food, and blow the last five dollars to decorate my new interior and tide me over until the first pay check would arrive for a job I had yet to find.

Four sweaty hours later, silver dollar sized blisters oozed on my heels; so I settled for a two-fifty a week basement hole and spent the rest of the day smearing yellow calcimine. Even in Heaven I might be on a stepladder from which I forever paint walls a cheery yellow and dream of casual, admiring friends.

Only one friend ever entered my nether paradise in Chicago, and I was so embarrassed by the stench of garbage cans outside my cellar window that I moved on Friday. My next home, located at the gloomy bottom of a three story air shaft, was so tiny that all four corners were within easy reach of my single bed. Still, I had to start entertaining sometime; so I invited a lonesome Mexican student to share a can of soup. I had a little trouble speeding that guest on his way, he was so comfortable. A man can easily get the wrong idea of a girl's intentions if her living quarters are nearly all bed.

Next I found an attic on Blackstone, a nice place with fresh air and room to stretch, but my acromegaliac landlady had nowhere to point her ever growing nose except into my business. She kept vigil at the newel post, her monstrous suffering face scaring me into another house hunt clear across the midway. I had two little jobs then and I thought I could afford a real apartment with a stove and sink. For a week I scrubbed the greasy overstuffed furniture with ammonia, before arranging my few dishes on the shelf and laying in a stack of vittles. I decided to bake a pie. I was rehearsing some suggestions for after class that I hoped would sound spontaneous.

"How about some coffee and pie over at my place?"

Or should I say a quick snack or a little bite? Should I select some odd-ball isolate or invite a whole chattering group? As I practiced, someone knocked at the door. How wonderful! Already I was having callers.

It was frowsty Mrs. Apartment Manager and she was gingerly holding out to me a paper bag. She spoke with averted face.

"I think it's a crying shame that I should have to speak to you at all about this, but we have children here in this building and decent people. I should think you would have more pride than to throw these things down the air shaft where everyone can see them."

Bewildered, I peered into the sack at a disgusting limp and sticky unmentionable, reacting at first with stiff indignation. "Why do you bring this to me? There are a dozen other apartments in this building."

"You're the only single girl. No one else would—."

Her curious assumption turned on my giggles, and she flounced away with a warning that there was nothing to laugh at or wouldn't be if it happened again. I could have withstood her sneering glance as I passed her sweeping the steps after that, because I was devoted to the gas stove, but then I saw the bed bugs, so I moved again.

Last Christmas Eve as I waited in a hospital emergency room for attention to a scratched eye, for want of something better to do, I listed all the moves I've made since college and I counted nineteen, excluding most of the temporary stays.

I've licked the stamps for Christmas cards at so many different addresses that it is no wonder my present rate of response is so low. When I think of all the stairs I've climbed with packing boxes, all the endless hours rearranging books and bedspreads, baby cribs and bureau drawers, I wonder why my pursuit of happiness couldn't have taken a less strenuous form. As kids we moved by hay wagon. One of my earliest memories is scrambling through the hedges along Euclid Avenue trying to catch the chickens who squawked loose when their crate fell off. In later years I often wished for a hay wagon, like the time I moved from 47th and the lake shore to 55th and Kenwood by rollaway bed. In those days of boundless energy, no carton of books was too heavy or any block too long, if I could gain a cleaner entry or a better view of the lake or some unique feature like a circle of flaming cannas outside my door.

One wintry day enroute to class I snatched a runaway toddler out of the street and returned him to his serious young mother, who was overloaded with grocery and books. That was how I met Anne and Ben, students with no income. You had to know someone important in those days to get a job peeling onions. Ben's influential parents were pulling cross-country strings to land their son a freight tossing job at the railroad terminal. Anne said that they'd found a peachy seven room apartment for forty-two fifty a month. If Ben started working and they could interest a few others in going with them, they wanted to move in.

I was more than willing to join up. Ben brought home another freight handler named Bernie, who needed lodgings for himself and his two year old daughter Norma while her mother decided whether she wanted freedom. We rented out the living room couch to Merle, an Ohio friend who was studying radio mechanics, and we were all set. Suddenly I was no longer alone and friendless but part of a busy commune, the young people from all around crowding the kitchen with their hearty appreciation of our food and their belly-filling schemes.

Ben would come home with a few oranges and a head of lettuce he'd liberated from a smashed crate, and Bernie would pull onions and sweet potatoes from his jacket pockets. Cook Annie gloated over each succulent contribution.

"This is wonderful, fellows. Usually I can't find any meat for less than fifteen cents a pound but today they had lamb shanks at two for a quarter; so I walked over to the bakery for a nickel's worth of stale cookies. We can have both dessert and salad tonight. Oh, I see you already found the cookies, Lennie."

Lennie, an enthusiastic student of abnormal psychology, hastily explained, "I wasn't conscious of opening the bag, Annie, honest. My right hand has developed a mind of its own and it reaches out for any food available without my knowing a thing about it."

Zelma, an intense Russian in international law, always thought her ideas superior. "Listen, you take a tea bag, see, let me show you. Got some scissors and a needle and thread? Yeah, you cut each bag in four sections, baste the sides together and you make four nice cups of tea.

And say, I found that if I buy a big fish, I can get three meals off it. I just run home at lunch and turn on the gas—."

Norman, another social worker, said he'd walked through the wholesale district, "and there was this guy telling me that they sweep out the tea bins and sell you a whole pound of tea dust for a dime. He says you have to let it settle."

Ben had made a valuable discovery on the street car. "Annie, I met this old lady that's on relief and she says cabbage is making her sick because they give her two shopping bags full every week at the surplus center. She wonders if you'd like to trade her our ham bones."

Annie shushed us then, because she wanted to hear Merle's rich baritone floating through the bathroom window which opened into the kitchen.

"What I'd like is a cake of soap," came the deathless words with full operatic flourishes.

Annie tossed him the Lava, our laboring men's favorite, while Zelma went over the fish story and I answered the door. It was Betty, an art student, with a small jar of peanut butter.

"I had a little bread but I was dying for peanut butter and lettuce sandwiches. I only had a dime. Do you please have a few lettuce leaves?"

In the meantime Norma and Anne's little boy, playing in the pantry, had unscrewed the pickle jar lid and everyone remembered their old craving for dill.

When 1939-40 drifted into oblivion and the good friends progressed to better living standards, I wrote to my parents who were still scuffling along on Bloody Run with the oil lamps and the ditch water. "Merle is marrying the blonde statistician from my office, Bernie and Norma are going home to his wife, Bennie and Anne are on their way to a job in Kansas; so now is your chance to get out of the woods and come to the city. There's plenty of room."

"By golly, we're going to do it," my mother wrote back. "We're sick and tired of this lonesome mudhole."

After they peddled the house on "land contract," they auctioned off the square grand piano, the oak sideboard, the horse collars and whiffle trees, Milton's trombone and the bread mixer, the short-chimneyed kerosene stove that leaked, the boot-jack and the fresh yellow cow; all of it netted the pitiful sum of fifty-five dollars, since a rainy November day is poor for drawing crowds. It was enough for train fare. My mother was absolutely thrilled with the city. When she wasn't revelling in hot running water and push-button lights, she sat in the front bay window watching the neighbors.

Within a week she knew that the shoe store manager across the hall was no uncle to the buxom cashier who shared his apartment, that the couple in the third floor flat in the second building down left their kids alone on Saturday nights, that the Swedish lady downstairs would be glad to lend us her curtain stretchers, and that the

Bohemian woman over there had slashed the tires of the family car to stop her husband going out with his fancy lady. I'd never known any of those things.

My father said he was sure he'd never had it so good. "I'd rather have one room here where I can get on the street car and see what's going on, maybe take in a ballgame or a show, than a whole farm back in Ohio. I'm going to see one of these construction outfits about a little watchman time and we'll be on Easy Street."

When spring came he talked about the good taste of a mess of dandelion greens and how pretty the radishes looked poking through the ground. He wondered whether old man Cuddeback had sold his bay mare and how the pear tree had stood the winter. He left one day saying he was riding out toward Joliet to find a farm where he could work, and the next thing we heard was a phone call from his sister in Cleveland, saying he'd appeared there acting confused and depressed. Aunt Olive thought my mother should come and see about him.

My mother cried all the way to the station. "I'm coming back," she promised. "First time in thirty years I ever had a decent place to live and he has to spoil everything. I'll fix him. He can go live in a soldiers' home."

Of course that was the end of city life for her. I gave up the apartment after one of those miserable failures at sharing with an irresponsible couple who never kept jobs because they stayed up so late they couldn't get up in the morning.

My last little home in Chicago was a two room rear building back of the stockyards. Meredith was just beginning to walk and I was determined that we should have something that would pass for a yard. I mastered the care and feeding of an oil space heater and enticed a bored caseworker away from her South Shore opulence to help me paint and paper. We were befriended by a Polish housewife who talked mostly about how she washed everything in the house weekly, including the window shades. That made me feel like a pretty slouchy housekeeper although our little place seemed homey. A motherless ten year old from the front house adopted us. She played games and sang lullabies to Meredith while I made cookies and remodelled old clothes into Sunday dresses for both the girls. We didn't mind much the occasional smell from the stockyards.

Then came the winter of 44-45. From every radio Bing Crosby warbled about how much he liked a white Christmas. Early in November the elements obliged. As if they had been turned loose by the winter god's foolish apprentice, the snowflakes never stopped falling. With the thermometer stuck around zero, ruts froze solid along the street car tracks. The space heater gobbled oil like a thirsty whale. North Pole winds howled and the snow kept falling. Each day began wrong, the baby moaning that she'd been deserted in her play pen whenever I fetched more oil from the tank under the house, the car refusing to start or to chug out of the drifts.

Sometimes we got under way after I charged off to work through the blizzard with the baby, her paraphenalia, my purse and slippery notebook, only to bounce off the ice into a snowbank. If there were no Samaritans abroad, and all altruists worked overtime that winter, we would catch a street car to the foster home where Meredith stayed daytimes, and then I would be hours late bringing us home again that night.

One bitter Sunday evening after a day of chills and fever, I took Meredith to her foster granny, went home to pull my couch closer to the heater and conked out, too sick for a week to worry about finding a doctor. That finished Chicago for me. I felt a great need to be among relatives who could help when life was too hard. I quit my job, sold the beds and table, and packed up the Terraplane.

Meredith seemed a little sick on the day I set forth; so I left her with Granny, planning to return for her by train. A few miles out of Chicago a sleepy truck driver demolished my four wheels and cherished goods. Not the type to dwell on bad luck, he barely slowed down, no doubt thinking that I wanted time to pull myself together. I had just located my unbroken glasses under the seat, laid them carefully on the running board and stepped on them, when a kinder truck driver stopped to help. I accepted his offer of a ride back to Chicago, too shaken to know my own name for a while, but the accident turned out to be a real break, since old jalopies were worth fortunes in war time and the insurance company paid off with a fifteen hundred dollar bundle. That gave us a grubstake for a new home in Ohio.

The first was a little four room brick on a street of identical new houses in which shy wild bushes grew through the cracks in the basement walls, and everything was too small except the bare clay yards. My parents lived with me, anxiously helping me calculate whether we could afford another load of topsoil after paying the storm window installments. In lively neighborhood competition I caught Improvement Fever. Since then I've had many courses of plumbing bill and home loan payment therapy as well as strenuous programs of lumber company shock treatments, but I'm still suffering from the same disease. I have seasonal attacks of paint spatters, high ladder palsy, and wall ripping out manias. Only the first deed was for a mass produced dwelling. Unique old houses lend themselves so much better to improvement.

When the War was over, my sister came home with a nest egg inherited from her last employer, and she bought the little brick house. Duane and I were living by that time in the dairyman's cottage on a rich man's estate. After Connie was born, we went house hunting on Sunday afternoons, searching for a country place with a good bit of land which wouldn't cost more than forty-five hundred, considering what we had for a down payment. A cottage on a wooded hill, two rooms with an iron ladder leading to an unfinished upstairs, appeared to yearn for us to be its owners, and we succumbed to its charms. First we gave it a stairway, then a kitchen addition with a furnace in one corner and cupboards of watermelon red. It wasn't perfect, though. We had a fine flowing well, but the water was ginger colored, and plumbing was reluctant; the septic tank gurgled sludge into our pretty babbling brook. With Duane working away from home the first year we lived there, the girls and I tried to solve problems ourselves. When the bathroom sink backed up, I fiddled with coat-hanger and plunger until I somehow dislodged the drain pipe under the house. The only person small enough to wriggle through the little hole in the foundation was Connie, three years old and pretty sure she didn't like the idea.

"I bet there's snakes under there, and spiders."

"Oh, nonsense. I can see all around with a flashlight and there's nothing scary at all. It's clean and dry." I hoped I sounded reassuring.

"Well, maybe you could bribe me," Connie offered, "but not with money. I don't need any more."

We closed the deal with three bedtime stories, a gray kitten, scrambled eggs with ketchup on demand, and no more vegetable soup. In just a few minutes her clever little fingers succeeded, but the drain still didn't work, and a whole procession of septic tank experts was required, each one hinting not so delicately that the former bandit should have had his head examined for using so little gravel and so short a trench. There is nothing adorable about any septic tank contractor, but I did admire the honesty of the grouch who held out the bill he'd discounted from the original robbery.

"Twon't last. You'll have to keep digging. This hardpan clay works just like a bathtub. Fill her up and she overflows." His manner was as sour as an overworked leech bed.

Plumbers have never inspired my devotion either, but carpenters are another story, with the excitement of their ringing hammers and the perfume of sawed wood. Duane and I planned for two years how we would build a new living room panelled with red oak and wild cherry from our own woods. We felled the trees, and snaked them out of the woods on the first crusty snow; they lay heaped in the front yard for a year. Through another four seasons we gloated over the rose tinted lumber, before the chips began to fly under the careful hands of our personable Finnish carpenter, Walter. He recited "The Cremation of Sam McGee" while he set the roof beams and quoted Wordsworth while he shingled the roof. He was such a cheer radiator that Duane's melancholy conviction about the depravity of mankind broke up temporarily like a January thaw. I helped hoist roofing nails and tar paper up the ladder, and Meredith concocted coffee cakes for our refreshment breaks up on the ridgepole.

The most nearly merry times of our usually grim marriage were shared projects on that house. One midnight as the work progressed, we took a notion to switch the places of front door and window, and were driving the last nail next morning just as Walter reported early for work. He good-naturedly offered to cover our mistakes. The little house grew into a four bedroom poor man's palace with a rough fireplace fashioned from pinky beige stones we dug out of the riverbed. Duane suggested that we paint the exterior coral and I was delighted. In that part of my heart where I carry house memories, there is an unfadable picture of our warm bright house against the forest green trees, blossoms from a snowball bush sprinkling the lawn.

In that same loved woods Duane shot himself a few years later when life became intolerable for him.

We had to sell the house. A poor excuse for a handyman, I lost the battle with septic tank and water softener, the snow clogged driveway and the cantankerous pump. New owners watched the sparks fly up our chimney, and we moved to town. Released from the bondage of trying to keep peace with a man who distrusted everyone, we threw open our home to college students and neighbor kids, including the children at the county receiving home a block away. Since this house obviously needed improving, I had the bright idea that the idle county wards could help me and earn spending money by tearing off the old wall-paper. They set to work before I left for the office in the morning and I nipped cross-lots at noon to see how they were doing. For some strange reason, the house was hidden in a cloud of dust. My eager assistants thought paper stripping too tedious; so they had sledge-hammered off every bit of plaster in one room and were starting on another. Repairs cost so much that I knew I would never have any savings anyway, and borrowed to convert the back porch into a panelled study.

The house throbbed with intimate talks about love, lousy parents, college intrigues, and e.e. cummings. One night as a Chinese student was telling me how it felt to be the kind of man no one wants his daughter to marry, I got claustrophobia. Bobby Wong felt it too; so we knocked down the dining room wall. By morning we had a more workable kitchen for those times when the whole play cast of the community theater came over for food.

An enchanting frequent guest was Cindy, the emotionally deprived pretty daughter of a wealthy Easterner. She tried to immerse herself in what she deemed the warm and loving culture of the poor, to keep her sane during the next bitter vacation wrangle at home. There were eighteen of us twisting sphagetti around our forks at the table one evening. Half a dozen neighbor kids perched on the window sills listening to the table talk, and three silent pre-school waifs squirmed among the diners to rest their noses on the table edge. Cindy was telling us about her favorite fantasy.

"All my life I've dreamed that my parents would go on a trip somewhere and never be able to come back. I wouldn't want anything bad to happen to them. Maybe they could get caught behind the iron curtain. Then I could live with poor foster parents and have a nice, ordinary life."

In the ensuing silence while a few of us contrasted our own wake-up-rich fantasies, a shrill agonized squeak filled the air. It seemed to come from under the sink. Ten year old Tommy investigated. "It's a mouse with his head caught in a ventilating hole and he can't go either way. I'll fix him."

Tommy dashed home and we soon saw him cycling at full speed toward us to the whistled tune of the William Tell Overture, a beebe gun across the handlebars.

"Don't hurt him! Don't hurt the poor little mouse," Cindy begged.

Tommy took aim. "Are you nuts, Cindy? It's a MOUSE!"

Tommy shot.

Cindy collapsed in grief, the others in laughter, and the anonymous infants took advantage of the confusion to snatch the biscuits and beat it for home.

In many ways that house had everything we wanted, but my job at the welfare department deteriorated into warfare, and in high spirits of idealism, many of us resigned. I had been there fourteen years and thought I was indispensable, but that was another illusion. A little

numb from sudden change, when I hunted work I un-
wisely chose two part time positions in Akron and Cleveland, which meant that my third job was commuting,
and the girls took care of themselves.

It seemed sensible to give up our good time house and
move to Cleveland. Across the hall from our spacious
fourth floor walk-up lived Joanne and Faye, outspoken,
humorous sisters. Leaving our doors unlocked to con-
nect the twelve rooms made it much easier to check each
other's refrigerators when we ran out of milk and eggs.
Since we had so much room, we took in college students,
all of whom had friends. The fourth floor quivered with
jollity, somewhat to the annoyance of the folks downstairs. In an effort to improve building relationships, we
invited everyone to a potluck supper in the courtyard,
and all sixteen families turned out.

There was a Filipino doctor, a Korean nurse, and a
sad old Jewish mother who had promised her sons she
would support them as long as they stayed in school. The
boys were with her, crafty lads of thirty-seven and thirty-
eight. We hadn't known any of them existed.

And there was Sharon, a blue eyed girl with a husband
and whimpering baby and the dazed look of a nightmare
rider. Sharon needed to talk. During the following
months, she poured into our collective ears the story of
her husband, which began when she was a mid-western
waitress, an inexperienced girl who'd never heard of
Freud. "I worked the late shift and this musician started

coming in after concerts. I felt sorry for him. He was always alone and he seemed shy and such a gentleman. He took me home and never laid a hand on me. He said he wanted to get married right away, and I didn't know how to say no. There wasn't anyone else who ever mentioned marriage."

Sharon burrowed between the sofa cushions to find the baby's pacifier and through the coffee table litter for cigarettes. She never had much heart for housework.

"He said we'd have to live in a hotel because he travelled so much, and I thought it would be fun for awhile except that he was hardly ever there, but he said he was always practicing and I didn't know. He finally took me to meet his mother, but when we got out of the car, he didn't seem to want to go in. Finally he asked me not to say anything about being married because he was afraid it would upset his mother."

"D'you mean to say that the creep had never left home?" Joanne demanded. "Can you dig a guy sneaking off from his wife to sleep at mother's! Come on, Sharon, tell us how you got him to act like a husband."

Sharon blushed. "He wasn't so bad about that, except he didn't know much and he was always in such a hurry."

"Well, he was in love, wasn't he?" Faye asked.

Sharon talked as if the Horace she married had ceased to exist. But at the memory of that time when she still hoped he was a real man, she was close to tears. "No,

I got it out of him after a while. He was so touchy and queer and drank so much that the orchestra leader told him he'd have to see a psychiatrist or lose his job, and he claims the doctor told him that he could take his choice of getting married or cracking up, and I was the only girl he knew."

Sharon took over the thankless task of breaking the news to Mother, who was very upset indeed. That gave Horace reason to insist that they move home with her, and that was sheer hell. "She wouldn't let us sleep. She kept making Horace move from bed to bed until she had him on a couch in her room because she said he needed his rest and I shouldn't begrudge him that. I was so glad when he was let go from the orchestra in Kansas City, and we had to move to Cleveland. But he still says he's gotta go home every summer."

We had the good fortune to meet Mother when she came visiting at Christmas. Since we understood it was her function to separate Sharon and Horace, we were puzzled when she offered to baby-sit on New Year's Eve so the young couple could go out for a good time. Since Horace didn't know what fun was, they came home early. We heard them knocking at their door, then pounding and shouting, and we all looked over the bannister to see what was wrong.

Horace was so worried he actually spoke to us. "We can't get any answer. The doors are bolted and there are no sounds at all."

Meredith and her fiance ran down with a hammer and helped Horace smash the bathroom window. They found the baby huddled in a drugged sleep by the front door and mother knocked out with sleeping tablets. Next morning Mother was bitterly indignant, saying the whole episode was a plot of Sharon's to humiliate her. She packed and departed, and incredibly the snivelling Horace went along. He returned after six weeks in worse shape than ever.

We suggested the Family Service Association, but Horace wouldn't go.

When we moved to Virginia, Sharon said good-bye by wrapping her arms around my neck and sobbing wildly. I was deeply moved, realizing that in gaining immunity to the grief of my own farewells, I had almost forgotten how it feels to be deserted.

For our luxurious trip south, the college where I was to teach paid the expenses. They asked if we could kindly pack our breakables to save money; so we did, but the professionals said they couldn't be responsible for breakage unless they repacked. It was a treat to watch them tenderly wrap the cracked jelly glasses, the full sugar bowl, and finally their own cigarette remains in the ash tray. Never since have my chattels been handled so well.

In 1962 college professors I knew had little money to redecorate houses. One man told me that he wouldn't have had a suit to wear to lectures if it hadn't been for the gift from his retarded brother who helped out around a gas station. Since we weren't fixing up the rented house, Connie and I wandered around the city seeking beautiful vistas. At the end of a side street islanded with flowering dogwood, we found a breath-taking overlook. Far below, the James River glistened, and across the horizon stretched the mysterious blue mountains.

"How much would you give to live here?" Connie had been exploring. "That little red house is for sale. It's empty and just happens to have an open window."

Lavender wisteria trailed across the leaded windows. A cocky weather vane twirled on the silver roof, and we followed an inviting path down the hillside to the open window. Not little at all, the house rambled crazily in all directions. We had to have it. Since it belonged to another professor who was anxious to unload, we took over with no down payment just when daffodils erupted all over the hills. We were barely able to sleep nights for fear of missing a moment of its surrounding beauty. Located in the city, it had all the seclusion of the wilderness and had been empty so long that the wild things thought they owned it. Bunnies pranced across the porch. An angry little scorpion goosestepped under the door, set its dainty front feet on my textbook of social problems and switched its little blue tail in exasperation at so much over-population. An indigo bunting serenaded from the top of a leafless black pillar. We loved every inch of the place, forgiving its sins of crumbling porch, precipitous yard, no shower and encroaching rear jungle. We threw our energies into freeing the jacqueranda from the loathsome kudzu vine and clearing paths down to the river where we kept a kayak.

College students turned the house into the local youth hostel, with political discussions raging all night between northern radicals and southern conservatives, the debaters often calling for reinforcements from the dorms. Usually I knew the visitors, but one morning I woke and saw a young man none of us could recognize asleep on the living room couch. He finally roused and explained that some girl from a nearby college had been visiting at Davidson in North Carolina and assured him that he could stay at our house if he would drive her home. We didn't even know the girl.

Our house began attracting unwelcome attention from local bigots who were terribly concerned that some of our friends did not have white skins. We received anonymous threats of arson, and strangers began shouting obscenities at us from cars swinging fast around the end of the street. It made me a little nervous. I began considering an investment in door keys, which had not been included when we bought the house, but then the bigots made their pitch with our college president, and it hardly seemed worth while to lock doors after I'd lost my job.

There will probably never be another house like that for me or for others who lived there. Former residents of fifty years back stopped in to see it once more, but it was very hard to sell when I had to leave. In the end I had to give it to a woman who agreed to stand good for the mortgage payments if I would co-sign so that she could borrow money for the closing costs.

"I'll never buy another house," I vowed through farewell tears.

I did though. In Washington I played the game again, tearing out walls, hating plumbers, loving carpenters, painting the kitchen yellow, the whole ritual. For a time I went so far as to dream that I might make the old place a Capitol Hill restoration display. But after taking one of the tours, I knew I could never compete with the bachelors who spent seven years of their spare time hand rubbing the old woodwork, or with the crank who found exactly the right spot in a bay window for a six hundred year old coffin of a Chinese child.

I could tell when I was licked; so Meredith agreed to take over for me and I escaped in that old camper across country, discovering happily that I didn't need my own fenced patio when Uncle Sam furnishes such fine picnic groves and camping spots for my pleasure. There are towns in North Dakota and Oregon where the city is so hospitable that they furnish free electricity for visiting campers too. I like that. There must be quite a lot of old Pete Crawford in me.

I did eventually find a town in which to settle down again, part of the attraction being a dear little shack of three rooms on which I can pay the smallest rent in the country, a shack so expendable that the landlady doesn't care what I do to it. So far I have enclosed the little porch to have a spot for a fireplace and installed a five dollar bathtub from the junkyard. There are still a few remodelling tasks. I can find most of the necessary materials .at the dump, and all kinds of free things come in handy. I plan to write more about this present homeplace, but I can't right this minute because I'm building concrete and flagstone steps down to the creek, and the mortar might set up too hard if I don't hurry.

PEOPLE HELPING

9

Miss Cora Loomis, whose brown eyes could snap as loud as her supple fingers, passed along with me from the third-fourth grade combination to the fifth-sixth; so I had her insistent urges that I amount to something for four years, a circumstance that suited both of us pretty well until the day she shamed me. We were supposed to be writing stories, and mine was one page, the least I could get away with before diving into my library book to race across the fields of Sunnybank with one of Terhune's collies.

"Ellen, I'm surprised at you. I thought you wanted to be a writer."

I put away the book and knocked out another tale, which Miss Loomis said was not bad although it sounded a little familiar. If I'd ever heard the word, I could have told her it was derivative. I was working alphabetically through the whole library fiction section to see how the others did it,—Jane Austen, Arnold Bennett, Willa Cather, Farnol, Galsworthy— That was as far as I had got, with side trips into other shelves.

It's a good thing I didn't demand such polished preparation to begin earning my living, or I would have starved to death. I did have faith that a college education would prepare me for being a big spender on my own easily earned money, but it wasn't a dedication to the ideal of fitting myself for a career that drove me, but the simple desire to live someplace where they had bathtubs.

Besides, my mother and her sisters thought a nice office job in some business would be just the thing for their daughters. Cousins Martha, Anna, and Edna did very well after a six months' course in typing and short-hand, and I was gloomily expecting that some old clumsy Remington in a sooty Cleveland office would be my life's companion too.

"It's nice clean work," my mother pointed out. "Lots better than washing dirty diapers for somebody else's kids."

But I was saved from that eternal boredom by a flukey stroll around the high school one spring noon. There'd been a home room announcement that after lunch we were to choose among the courses the school offered. These were "college prep" for the rich kids, "general" for the misfits, and "commercial" for the sensible. As I walked with my sarcastic friend Alice, I ate my jelly bread sandwiches, and we mourned the necessity of sign-ing away our youth and freedom for the commercial route to a livelihood.

"At least we won't have to take algebra and geome-try," I said consolingly.

Alice could always spot a weakness. "What makes you think we could pass business math?"

I tried again. "Look at the nitwits who do pass."

Alice was pretty depressed too. "Our handwriting is terrible, but that won't let us out, because we'll be *typists* , sitting on those dinky chairs for nineteen hours a day."

I offered her a cookie. "Listen, Al, we don't have to worry. No one would hire us anyway."

Alice suddenly jumped as if she'd stepped on a hot wire. "Are we dumb! I've got it! You know who is graduating from high school this year? Our big brothers. In four years they will be so rich they can send us to college."

With that silly solution we elected college prep,—algebra, Latin, science and all. We had a laughing wild four years, while the girls in the commercial course gradually faded out.

So did our big brothers!

Alice's candidate for affluence ran away to get married before he graduated. You had to run away in those days. Any late twenties parents who saw that their kids were hopelessly lovesick filled up the gas tank of the family flivver and laid maps to Ripley, New York, in conspicuous places. No one had the money for gowns and wedding cake. My brother Milton tried selling razor blade sharpeners, solid rubber chunks for stuffing tires, crystal sets, and electroplating correspondence courses, before he gave himself up to President Roosevelt's CCC.

Alice and I went to college anyway with some delays. We were committed.

I said I was going to be a teacher. That was before I sat through Education I, II, III, and IV, which was like a full course dinner of bean soup, each succeeding dish containing more water. So then, with a careless disregard for my future, I transferred to Liberal Arts.

"How do you make a living at that?" my mother worried.

"Well, I'm studying sociology."

The family asked what the heck that was. I hurried through some vague description. "Listen, I've got these great professors, and they say I can get a job as a social worker."

"What in the world is a social worker?"

It must be a significant aspect of our changing times that no one in all our poverty had ever known a social worker. No one ever filled in our face sheet, verified our earnings and calculated our budget, or any of those other helpful things I later did for penniless Americans. The nearest our family came to a handout was the time the Nickel Plate Railroad paid my father forty dollars for the horse that wandered across the tracks. My father was so electrified by the unexpected fortune that he invested five of the dollars in another nag, but he never had the heart to do more than sprinkle hay in the general direction of the locomotives.

As I began my full time people-helping career in 1939, armed with identifying information about a hundred miserable Chicago families and a handful of street-car tokens, I asked my supervisor for last minute help. "Do I have to give them much advice?"

She clutched her blonde mop with both hands, shrieking, "Advice! What advice do you know how to give? Check their eligibility as courteously as possible. That's all."

I began quite humbly asking to see the light bills and rent receipts and birth certificates, but when one ignorant child-producer ranted about how hard she whipped five year old Samuel because he was so bad, I couldn't resist asking if she ever praised him.

"I just told you he don't do nothing I can praise him for," she lamented; so I let it go. A month later, when she said that she'd tried my suggestion and Samuel was a changed child, I continued carrying my candle light of change into the bedbug harbors and urine drenched tenements.

It was a truly hellish occupation. What we were really supposed to do was sit by the sewers in which the clients were kept, watch to see if anyone got his fingers on the edge of the manhole and then smash him so he could never get out. A really sharp fraud-sniffer knew how to proceed.

"I notice you have new curtains, Mrs. Smith. How did you pay for them? A friend? You'll have to give me his name and address so I can verify this information."

"You say you haven't worked since 1936, Mr. Washington, and your landlord has let you stay all this time without rent? Oh, odd jobs. Well, tell me exactly where and when. You'll have to prove every cent, or we can't issue your next check."

"Let's see now. You say that Billy quit school because he could earn fifteen dollars a week parking cars. That's wonderful, if he wants to help out like that. We can allow him car fare and two dollars a month for lunches away from home, and the rest we'll have to take off your budget; so your family check will be fifty-one dollars next month."

There were some of us who fudged reports, like my friend Fred Jay, who played his harmonica so the thin children could dance, before he went back to the office and invented answers. That was taking grave chances, since the administrator hired squads of checkers who were expected to file against a certain percentage of chiselers every month.

My friend Duke said he kept the fraud department lads busy by referring all clients who wore stockings.

"Only the sockless are really honest," he pointed out. "They don't have knitting machines at the sewing centers."

That was true. WPA sewing centers weren't financed for fancy work. The poor could have plenty of white muslin underwear, flannel shirts and crib sheets, but no stretchy things at all. People should have been grateful, the newspapers yelled, but clients kept complaining. Some people wanted extraordinary things.

"I just wanna eat on Christmas Day," Sadie Watkins wailed. "I know the W checks come out on the 28th. They don't need to pay no caseworker to tell me that, but why can't they give me mine on the 24th, just this one month? I don't care if I go hungry six days in January. Maybe I'll be dead then anyway."

Janet Prince was more interested in staying alive. "The doctor at the clinic said I should take a pill after every meal, and I asked him how I could do that when I ain't got no meals, and he said he couldn't answer that. Now you tell me. I want to live to be an old lady like the rest of the family."

She wasn't comforted by my explanation that single people could have only seventeen dollars a month, even if their room rent was twelve since there wasn't any more money to go around, but she forgave me my powerlessness and she died before my next visit. Most of the dying people were kind.

Sam Jones, and I use his real name on purpose, crocheted a string chair-back for me. He knew that caseworkers were forbidden to accept anything at all from clients, but he brushed aside my refusal. "You just take this and say nothing. I've been saving all the string I could find to make this for you. It didn't cost a cent but my time and nobody needs that. I want you to remember old Sam Jones. Won't anyone else ever remember him."

Then he went on to scold me for the asinine suggestion I'd made that he take in a room-mate to help pay the rent. "No, mam, I ain't shared my bed with no one but a lady since I been growed and I ain't starting now."

Many hours of my life have been spent as a worker in child welfare with pregnant irregulars who needed housing and jobs, medical care and adoption agencies. Informed once that a "funny looking" woman wanted to see me, I had the luck to meet Bernette. She was an inspiring example of courage. Dressed in any old thing and not believing in marriage after the first sad attempt, she still thought sex could be a comfort if you were poor. That was thirty years ago, and Bernette was too bright to advertise her views in the little religious town where she was bringing up her child and caring for her invalid parents. No one noticed that another child was growing inside her camouflaged body, and she paid the doctor by baby-sitting money earned after she put her own family to bed. I wondered how she could manage hospital time.

She said that was no problem. Late one night she asked her only trustworthy neighbors to run her to the hospital and help her parents until she returned from her emergency appendectomy. Two days later she was home again, calming the anxious nurses with a breezy, "Listen, I'm nobody's pampered wife."

Every week for six months after that, she sneaked away long enough to visit her bright eyed son and pour a heap of nickels and dimes on my desk to pay for his board. Adoption placement often took a long time, because of agency rules that we match the religious sects of the concerned parties. Meanwhile, Bernette fussed at me that the baby should know his new parents as soon as possible. After the adoption was final, she still checked on how he was getting along, and came in quite breathless when he was three years old to remind me that he needed an eye exam because her family was near sighted.

Few girls were that clear headed. There was Virginia, who kept regular counselling appointments with me, which I found was quite gratifying, since most maternity home residents considered their problems solved once they entered the sheltering doors. Virginia wallowed through her love troubles with Buster, considering whether his AWOL jaunts, his interest in other women, and his failure to support her indicated lack of stability, or whether she ought to appreciate being introduced to a more free life style. Should she return to Petersburg and Buster after she delivered, or strike out for herself?

One day she pleaded, "Mrs. Moore, what shall I do?"

So help me, I thought she really wanted my opinion.

"Virginia, there's one thing I'm sure about. You should not go back to Petersburg unless Buster shapes up."

She dropped her eyes and ended the session, deeply impressed with my wisdom. A few hours later she called to meet me around the bend of the stairway, her face radiant, a girl all put together at last.

"Mrs. Moore, I've made a decision. I'm going straight to Petersburg. Aren't you pleased? I decided this all by myself."

Maternity homes were built and operated on some amusing assumptions. Unwed mothers and their parents expected that care would be free to unfortunates seeking admission, while staff and trustees threw around the contemptuous phrase "trying to get away Scot free" as they pointed to the rising upkeep costs of institutions. Girls, naive about social trends, braced themselves for lectures about immorality. Even the religious homes had abandoned that approach. Instead, the girls were tongue-lashed for eating. There was no greater sin in maternity homes than gaining weight,—even slipping out to the woods to meet boy friends, since one need no longer fear pregnancy. The staff was always uncomfortably doubtful, though, about whether a girl who had been gone for an unexplained hour needed another vaginal smear.

After the delivery took place, and a girl could again become pregnant, the staff's attitude changed drastically. Now they shared the girls' pious hope, "This time I've learned my lesson."

That was translated to mean "No more sex without marriage." Bitter fights raged among the staff about whether we should admit kids whose hurry-up marriages weren't succeeding. Married girls could too easily destroy the "happy ever after" illusion. Second offenders were another controversial category.

Most of the girls were as much against a program of contraceptive information as were their parents and the trustees.

"You just can't teach contraception, as well as Christian restraint," one housemother admitted sadly.

"That would be planning to sin!" said a shocked nineteen year old, and I'm sure she didn't mean that spontaneous sin was more fun.

I've used the past tense about such discussions, since the practical lesson of "No more sex without contraceptives, or else the friendly family abortionist" has by now been too well learned, and the maternity homes are converting to old folks facilities. The change was so sudden that they got caught with their building plans down. Back in 1964 the business in unmarried motherliness was booming, and I rented a large house in order to shelter the countless worried girls who didn't have the proper conditions of singleness, youth, sanity, and advanced gestation for gaining admission to the established institutions. Over a period of two years, about seventy-five losers in love came to stay with me in what they sometimes called Moore University.

We didn't have a dishwasher or television or a hired cook; so everyone had to make do. Myrna said she'd never washed dishes in her life, since her mother wanted her to save her hands for the piano. Amanda struggled through our book collection and announced one day, "Hey, you know what? I've learned to read!"

A girl named Jannie said, "The important thing I've learned is not to be married first, if you get yourself into this kind of fix." Jannie's husband was overseas when she met his cousin, and they had a long talk about war and poor old Dave. Neither of them were proud of the form their mutual consolation took, but the adoption agency was adamant about the legal necessity for Dave's signature, since the child was technically his.

At our house, everyone took courses in obstetrics, family relationships, cross-cultural conflicts, and the art of hiding out. Dinner table conversation was as spirited about the pronunciation of house (southern or New England?) as it was about the practicality of taking an interracial baby back to Wisconsin. In the usual maternity home they never had to face the problem about how to tell your married children that you'd got yourself pregnant, because they never took anyone over thirty-five. But at one time most of the girls were beyond that advanced age at Moore U.

"I couldn't believe it," said fifteen year old Beth. "When I came here, I thought you must be having all the neighbors in for tea."

The older residents found it just as shocking that they had been caught. It was bitter knowledge that this had happened when one was no innocent adolescent but old enough to know better. Some of them had already learned that there is no wise age. But not Marie, because until her forties, she'd been a happy old maid with a good job and congenial friends but no lovers. However, like most women she cherished a secret hope that the right man would still come along. Then a candidate did appear, a man with the same vocational and recreational interests but also with the same wariness about marriage. When Marie became pregnant, he shuddered at the idea of legalizing their responsibilities. Marie hysterically considered suicide, before coming across town to hide with us and serve her sentence.

About midway in my long career of people-helping, I wondered how often it was people-harming. One morning I collected two forlorn girls from the receiving home, and tried to spruce up their spirits for the juvenile court hearing.

Twelve year old Rose with the fear-bombed eyes couldn't respond to the old cheerio. "I think I'll run away again right now. What's the use? That old judge will just send us home, same as he did last time."

Nettie slipped her crooked right arm, the one her father often kicked out of sight, through mine. "Please don't let him get us again. He'll kill us the next time."

"You don't need to worry," I said. *I*, the experienced social worker, the protector of the abused and neglected, the compassionate public servant who understood the intricacies of Ohio justice. "The judge always tries to give parents another chance, because he knows that everyone makes mistakes, but he already sent you home once. This will be different."

Half an hour later, the triumphant father herded his terrified daughters out to the family pick-up, while I, the betrayer and the betrayed, scratched the eczema on my impotent hands. I cried at the judge: "How could you? How could you!"

The judge snapped shut his brief case. "You social workers get all worked up. My father beat me all the time and I lived to grow up, none the worse for it, either."

After another year of beatings, Rose and Nettie ran off again and then their father decided he could find less troublesome stoop labor; so the judge let me have them. But I never could find foster parents who shared my affection for those mistrustful, devious girls. They were not at all receptive to the abundant life, since they could never stop yearning for the parental love they'd never known. Nettie gave birth to a little boy and confided seriously that she planned to take him home to Daddy because "he'd love being a grandfather." But Daddy was not pleased. In frustration, Nettie beat her little son pretty badly before she gave him up for adoption "to some family who will never in his life make him pull weeds."

Rose set out on a different path to the same neurotic goal, marrying an infantile and sadistic young man whom she tried to love into health. Instead, he murdered her in a tantrum. Before they led him away to the penitentiary, the young widower told me, "Put my kids somewhere so far I'll never find them, because I'm the kind of a son-of-a-bitch who'll kill them too if I get mad."

Rose and Nettie's remorseful father came to see me then, not quite drunk enough to dull his pain. "You always said I didn't understand my kids. Maybe I didn't, but I was only trying to make good girls out of them, and I never treated them the way my father did me. He'd string me up in the garage by my thumbs and beat me unconscious, and God knows I deserved every bit of it. But you never gave me any help!"

It was true. I hadn't tried to help him understand how to be a father, because I had assumed he was hopeless.

And I caught a second glimmer of truth. We were all in the people-helping business, the judge, the tragic father and his daughters and I, all of us in accord with our ungolden rule. "Do unto others as has been or should have been done unto you."

But it takes more than a glimmer of light to see by, and I went right on functioning as if everyone I met was the tow-headed Crawford girl who'd never been spanked in her life.

There was a blowsy and tough Mrs. Hooligan who told me so pitifully how her husband mistreated her. "He knew we didn't have a bite of food in the house and he promised he'd bring something, but he never showed up. The kids and I went to bed hungry, and then about midnight he comes rolling in, and first thing I know he's blacking my eye by pelting frozen hamburger and onions at me. And why? He was that mad I didn't have his supper ready."

Could any woman stay with a man like that? Certainly not. I spent weeks househunting for the woman and her seven peculiar kids so she could make a fresh start. She seemed somehow lacking in enthusiasm, although always glad to see me, and at last I got the message. Mrs. Hooligan didn't want my help! She only wanted an audience, someone to admire her fortitude, her good humor under fire, and her dramatic presentation.

Once I manipulated the environment like pulling taffy to help a woman who was leaving her husband to establish a separate home for herself and her children, thereby delaying by several months her secret plan to let the old man have the little prigs since they thought he was such a saint.

I knew another caseworker who went all out for pretty clothes for a sullen girl who was then required to act grateful, when rags were what the girl really wanted, to enhance her role of orphan in the cruel world.

Then there was the psychologist who tried to coerce mothers into bottle-feeding their children because she was nauseated by the idea of breast feeding.

And then there was the minister who assumed that everyone who came for guidance was as impressed as he was with his bar-tending skill.

Social workers occasionally receive enough supervision to help them grow up, but nobody counsels the judges and parents and teachers and lawyers, who continue to dispense their raw ineffectiveness.

There are those who cannot understand who is making the mistakes. An aging principal told me, "The folks in this county will never learn. I taught the grandparents of these kids, and I can see that each generation gets dumber."

And some of us in middle-aged disillusion go back to school in order to change fields. Social workers become teachers, teachers go for psychology, psychologists for creative salesmanship (I knew one who went into cemetery lots), and ministers decide to become taxi drivers or bartenders. "In the beer joint," they explain earnestly, "you can really communicate with others. It's probably the only real communion left in the world."

It may be. At least it takes a few years before we realize that we're playing the same old games in a different ball park, and the change may tide us over until we can decently retire and take up our true life work, candle making, horse training, betting on greyhounds, writing.

It is sad, too, that you can start out an altruist running hard every day to catch a pay check, and if you live so long, end up like me, a hedonist without any pay coming in.

I also think it gets tiresome trying to change the world and other people, when we never have succeeded at changing ourselves very much. Besides, it gets lonesome.

One dentist said that he'd spent the best part of a year working on a patient's deformed mouth.

"And when I finally got him looking and smelling like a human being, the guy told me: 'I hope to God I never have to see you again.' "

A little girl named Cherry explained to me long ago that people-helpers must accept the fact that one gains few lasting friendships by being close to others in time of trouble. She came into my life as a charming little five year old who had worn out her welcome in her relatives' homes. They said she wanted too much attention, and they didn't know what to make of her. Cherry was a child with the rare ability to recognize and handle subtleties. She lived in the receiving home until I found what I thought would be good adoptive parents for her, but that didn't work out. Cherry was not the passive little doll these kindly but immature people wanted, as Cherry eventually had to explain to them.

"She was the one who comforted us," the incredulous would-be mother told me. "She said it would be better if she went back to the receiving home, and we shouldn't cry because everything would come out all right."

Cherry told me that she'd rather be my little girl after that, but we talked that over and she thought she could try again in another adoptive home. This time the relationship clicked, and the day came when I made my last visit to the poised little lady of seven. We had an affectionate and gay little tea party. Then Cherry kissed me and said, "I'm very glad you came, Mrs. Moore, and I don't want to hurry you away, but I'm learning to skate and the ice won't last forever."

10

Ever since that heavenly day when Dennis the Dandy walked out of our house for the last time, I've been trying to invent a little gismo that will make me an instant millionaire. It will look something like an alternator, will be attached over the heart of a prospective friend, and the indicator will turn blue if the candidate is a right one, and puce if he has villain potential. I can't think of an uglier sounding color than puce.

If only I'd had that thing perfected when Dennis arrived, so debonair, a nice guy disarming and full of low-keyed agreeableness! I explained to him that students who lived with us paid for both room and board. They could eat with Connie and me if they were there at mealtimes, or they could cook whatever they found later if they washed the dishes when they were finished. Dennis said he thought that was a fine arrangement.

"And I've signed up for two of your classes," he added, putting our relationship on a very chummy basis.

I believe he attended each class only once, but when grade time rolled around he was raging mad to discover that he rated two flunks.

"It's not my fault." He complained like a sneaky ten year old with his pockets full of stolen apples. "Mose said he'd take notes for me and do my term papers too, and he never did. That's the luck I have in friends."

That wasn't quite the way Mose remembered the discussion with Dennis, as he indignantly told me after class. "I never promised any such thing. All I said was that I'd let him see my notes when I thought he had to miss just once. I should write his papers yet? I got enough grief doing my own."

It was typical of the kind of distorted impressions Dennis carried around in his handsome head. After the first time, he never paid any rent and became very upset that I should be so discourteous as to ask him for it. He claimed that I had welshed on my promise to cook his meals whenever he wanted them. "And anyway," he sneered, "this dump isn't worth paying for. I can get a much nicer apartment up town for the same price."

"You do just that," I urged, "as soon as possible."

It was actually months before he was able to locate a landlord gullible enough to let him move in, and then it was an unfurnished place. I told him he could take along the bed he'd slept in free of charge for so many weeks, and he felt so kindly toward me for that generosity that he took without my permission a table lamp and a supply of bed clothes. I really liked that lamp too, but I was so glad to be rid of him at any price that I felt as if somebody had lifted the Pentagon off my back.

My other roomers felt the same way. John was near explosion point. "That guy is a thief. He's been sneaking off with all my shirts and underwear. I chased him clear over to the campus when my good green shirt disappeared, and I was going to tear all his clothes off, and you know what he had the nerve to tell me? 'Oh, you mean that green thing? I didn't think you'd get in a sweat about that. Well, you can have it back. It wasn't pressed very well so I borrowed one from Dan. You can go get yours out of his room in the dorm.' "

You had to give him the credit for wanting to look neat. Yes, Dennis was a nice dresser. The last time I heard of him was when I ran into the manager of a department store where I'd learned Dennis had found a job as floorwalker. I asked how the boy was getting along, and the manager's eyes popped. His face got so red I thought he would have a stroke.

"Do you know that—,—. I can't think of a word bad enough for such a scoundrel. Do you know what he did? He used my office, *my office*, feature that, as a dressing room in the morning. He'd plug in his razor and change his clothes, taking whatever he needed out of our very best stock, and then he'd leave his dirty clothes piled on my desk. I was never so happy in my life as I was on the day I fired him."

Yes, with chiselers like Dennis on the loose, we need all the help we can get with a device like a friendship meter. I never want to get stuck again. I've had it. Let me count the times. There was Flora the foul-minded damsel who spread distrust and hatred wherever she stepped, and there was Mrs. Pinty, the paranoid case-worker who spent all her time trying to line up clients and staff to be on her side against her imaginary enemies, and then there was—. I can't seem to remember any others right now.

Maybe I won't need that meter after all. In a life as long as mine, three bad apples in a hundred barrels isn't such a terrible record. And another thing which might account for the way I've dilly-dallied about this invention is the fact that I'd be a little leery of having that thing attached over my own heart. I haven't always been such a true blue friend myself.

I once dropped my good friend Jill who was loyal, witty, intelligent and fun to be with at any time, to go all out for a new girl, a bleak, humorless snip whose most developed feature was the ability to complain. I've never been able to understand that period of my history.

I'm a little clearer about my motives in failing the McCardle family, whom I met and liked as I went about making home visits in regard to school children's problems in Washington. In one school there was an eccentric principal, Mrs. Batty, who liked to believe that most of the students in her bailiwick were moronic delinquents. Mrs. Batty as well as 99% of her students was black, so it never occurred to me it was all a case of racial prejudice, and it took several weekly calls before I understood what was involved. Each time Mrs. Batty would parade ten or twelve miserable children that she'd parked along the walls of her office. She was especially vindictive about nine year old Halley McCardle, whose chief crime, so far as I could fathom, was to dance a few steps in the hall to relieve the boredom of standing in line. The principal's annoyance with Halley was so vigorous that she would sometimes snatch her out of the classroom and expel her for a few days on general principles, although the teacher faintly protested that Halley had been guilty of nothing but paying attention.

One day I interrupted Mrs. Batty's tirade against the students by saying, "I can see you have your hands full here, Mrs. Batty, but at least you can be proud that Halley and so many of the other children are very intelligent."

Clutching the edge of her desk, Mrs. Batty hunched forward and glared. "Intelligent! None of these children are intelligent, and that Halley has the lowest I.Q. of all of them. How could they have any brains? They're nothing but low-class slum dwellers. Their mothers and their fathers, if they have any, are barely out of the cotton fields."

I got the picture pretty clearly then and wondered why it hadn't percolated through my thick head before. If any of those benighted children or their parents had near-normal intelligence, there wasn't a wide enough gulf between them and their distinguished principal. No doubt she had thought it was obvious that she was of higher caste. This idea was both startling and disgusting; so I rose hurriedly and said I'd better be on my way to see Halley's mother.

"You can't go there," Mrs. Batty shrieked. "That woman is crazy. Your life would be in danger. She's a witch."

Convinced that if I could escape from one witch, I could take on another, I plodded across to the teeming housing project where Mrs. McCardle lived with her six youngest children in a fine new four bedroom apartment. All the families in that area were large and very poor, and when I saw how many were out playing in the muddy courtyard, I wondered how the school could have been so full. All the McCardle children were at home.

Mrs. McCardle removed two of the little urchins from a kitchen chair so that I could be seated. She had bright black eyes and a friendly smile and didn't seem at all witchy.

"I hope you aren't going to make me send the kids back to school today," she began. "It isn't safe when that old battle-axe is on the warpath. She puts the evil eye on them. I know the boys are hard to handle and Halley talks back sometimes, but even our little Jean who never gets into trouble comes home nervous as a cat when Mrs. Batty is after her."

She told me some of her wretched history that day, including the reason she had so many children.

"They'd already sent my husband up for a stretch when I got that way the second time, and found out that I had tuberculosis besides. The doctor at the clinic said I wasn't in any shape to be having so many babies, so I asked him could he tie my tubes as soon as I had Ernest, and he said he sure could. So there I was in the hospital thinking that after the next morning I wouldn't have to worry any more and might even live to raise the two I had. And then along about midnight the priest came in. Yes, I'm a Catholic. I still am, but you can't make me believe God would want a woman who's so sick she can hardly raise her head to go on having one kid after another, but that priest talked real mean that night. He got me so upset I cried and cried, and the next morning the doctor sent me home. He said he couldn't take a chance on a woman who might change her mind afterwards and sue him. So everytime my old man got out of jail, I'd have another. I've had nine so far and I'm not forty yet."

She'd had nothing much but trouble in life, no regular income of any kind until she was accepted on welfare, rotten housing, no one to depend on, and the children growing up wild.

"Maybe things will be looking up," I said. "At least now you have a good place to live."

She grinned. "Oh, sure, real nice. Come and see it."

The kitchen was equipped with a table and three chairs with stuffing bursting out of the ragged plastic. In the sunken living room was one lop-sided couch with a broken leg, a picture of Jesus on one wall and a plush hanging of three horses in a green field on another. One bedroom had a double bed with no sheets. That was all. In three of the rooms there wasn't a single stick of furniture.

"The welfare claim they got no beds and no money for stuff like that," she explained. "We're supposed to be lucky we got one for all of us. You should see how some of these folks are living. Come the end of the month they don't have anything to eat. It's bad enough to tell your own kids they have to go hungry, but turning away the neighbor kids day after day really gets me."

That day was the longest uninterrupted time Mrs. McCardle ever had to tell me what was on her mind. Halley was at home to keep the little boys corraled for a while, and they didn't know me so well, but after a half hour the fence broke and they were all over me. Five year old Andy, in particular, reached out in a frenzy of hope that perhaps here was someone who might save him from drowning in nothingness. Dragging me into the living room, he talked incessantly, pointing out each little detail of "my Jesus" and "my horses." The McCardle boys were not very welcome in school where there were already far too many hyperactive kids yearning for any kind of decoration in their drab lives. Andy never did settle down. Although I knew many other families just as needy, the McCardles became special, and I wanted very much to do something better than to just listen and look. I told one of the Dominican sisters about them, and she became their friend too.

I began sneaking bags of cookies past the other hungry kids in the courtyard, and one time I took them a set of plastic dishes that I had decided I could live without, and then I felt like crying as Halley lovingly arranged the treasures on perfectly empty cupboard shelves. Sometimes on Sundays I took the family to McDonalds for hamburgers and once we all went to the Oxon Hill Children's Farm in Maryland. When I called Mrs. McCardle to make the arrangements for Saturday morning she said doubtfully that she didn't know if the children had anything to wear. I said any old clothes were good enough for a picnic.

When I arrived there next day every one of those kids came dashing out to show me new pants or shirt or blouse, and their mother explained that she had taken some of her food money to go over to H Street and get into a crap game. She'd been pretty lucky, worried as she was to leave the kids alone with Halley, and made enough to buy a few items. It turned out to be a rather stilted picnic, but I could see that when kids get perhaps the only chance they'll ever have to take a ride in the country to see real live horses and pigs as well as people who didn't live in poverty, they can't go in rags.

Sister Evelyn went to the school and humbly asked if she could take the most obstreperous children over to a nearby church and tutor them, but Mrs. Batty wouldn't consider any plan that would prove her scorn of the children unjustified. So then Sister Evelyn opened a school for after school and Saturdays, and the McCardles attended that.

There is considerable strain being friends with families like the McCardles. It takes a lot more out of one than having supper parties and games with friends who enjoy the same affluent level of poverty that I live in. After I left Washington, I neglected writing, and only had one Christmas card from them. I did call when I was last back east and learned that little Jean dropped out of school at sixteen to have a baby, and that the little boys are as wild as ever. Plucky Halley is still trying to get some semblance of an education against all odds. I didn't go to see them because it would have meant a long bus ride and then quite a walk in the ghetto, and I wasn't about to tackle that on a winter day. That's the kind of friend I am. Sure, I love you. I'd do anything for you, but I can't come over tonight because it looks like rain.

I expect friendship can be classified as either temporary or permanent. Even Dennis, I suppose, could be called a very temporary friend, and I've had some that didn't even last one day. Though it wasn't his fault. He was a pleasant young lawyer that I met through the services of a very hostile burglar who dropped in on us.

It was about eleven at night and I'd gone to bed upstairs while Meredith was asleep in her basement apartment. What woke me was the sound of breaking glass and loud voices that seemed to come from downstairs. Connie had gone away to finish college, and her friend Chuck was living with us. I wondered vaguely if he might be having a party, although he'd never done that before. Creeping quietly to the stair railing, I peered over to see a shabby stranger huddled on the floor against one wall. Then a voice yelled, "For God's sake call the police."

I obeyed, explaining to the lads at the precinct that I didn't really know what was going on but was only doing what I'd been told, and they said they'd send somebody right over. Again I obeyed when the voice came again.

"Did you get them? Come on down now and take this other gun."

Shivering in front of the broken front window, wearing nothing but his underpants and a pistol, was my next door neighbor Walt. He described to me how he'd actually seen this guy climb onto Walt's porch, located a foot from ours, kick in our window and climb through. Walt barefooted right after him and was holding the criminal until the police could arrive, but he was becoming nervous because all he'd been able to get out of the burglar was the suggestion that he had an accomplice outside. When the police came, they hauled the man off, although he had craftily refused to give his name or any other information about himself. Other neighbors came over to board up the window, and Walt's wife brought him a robe and shoes so he could walk home.

Booked as John Doe, the burglar was brought up for indictment before the judge, who might have been John Sirica since it was his name on the docket, and here the name of Giles came out when the judge said he was very glad at last to get a look at John Doe who had committed so many crimes around town. However, break-ins were so common then, and the court docket so crowded, that the case dragged on. Walt went to New England with his family and I moved West, without hearing another word about the District of Columbia versus Giles. More than two years later, I was back in Washington to see Meredith, when the phone rang. It was someone from the United States attorney's office requesting information about me.

Since I surprisingly proved to be so handy, they asked me to come down to one of the Federal buildings and go over the facts of the case again. I went because I thought it might be interesting to see the wheels of justice turning.

"This case will be coming up in July," the lawyer told me.

"But I'll be back in Arizona by that time."

"No problem. We'll fly you back and pay you twenty dollars a day plus expenses. Can you beat that working?"

Well no, at the time I certainly couldn't, since all I was making as delivery wagon driver was one sixty an hour, and I had no objection to another trip to Washington, but I still protested the expense to the taxpayers.

"But the guy didn't get one cent. Is it really worth while to spend all this money prosecuting? Where has he been all this time? Surely not in jail for more than two years."

The attorney laughed. "In jail part of the time and St. Elizabeth's Hospital a good bit, but you don't need to feel sorry for this bird. He escaped from a security ward in St. E's and they picked him up again for breaking into the White House. Besides, whether he stole anything or not is hardly the point. I was told to clean up these old cases no matter what it costs."

He was most likeable, and I looked forward to another chat with him about crime and social problems after a free plane ride, but in the end I didn't have the chance, because the defendant agreed finally to plead guilty to another charge if they would drop this one.

One of Connie's pals from elementary school I remember often with fondness. Mike was a husky bumbling youngster of fourteen who liked to pretend he was an ape with a broken elbow. Somehow he could dangle an arm as if it were hanging from a single tendon. The girls thought he was such a comic that he got carried away with his own boisterousness once and knocked a pitcher off the table. Contrite, he asked if he could do something to pay for the breakage since he never had any money. We'd just had a donation from the street department of a load of logs, and I asked Mike if he could split them. I couldn't have come up with a better treat for him. Mike was full of frustration and he seldom had a chance in his grandmother's knick-knacky home to let loose. With blazing glee in his eyes and a ringing shout of "Zowie", "Powie" or "Zap", he brought the axe up and over his head with all his strength. I've never learned to split wood, and there's a pile of logs out back right now. I'd gladly sacrifice another pitcher to have Mike return, but he's been gone a long time into his future, that mysterious world that lies ahead for all of us.

Lee was another friend I never see anymore, although I assume he still lives in some suburb around Atlanta. He never was much of a writer, most of his inventive genius going into oral creations. We met when we were both in a play at a college community theater. Learning that the new cast member was from Atlanta, I sought him out to ask if he knew Dr. Carl Whittaker.

His eyes gleamed and his handshake was hearty. Obviously if two people knew Whittaker, that gave them a close bond. "Of course I know him. My dad was one of his patients."

We were off on a running start in a fun relationship that lasted for the years Lee was in our town. He enjoyed my sister and my children and the other funny people I knew, becoming an enthusiastic member of what we called The Pauper's Picnic. The way it worked was that any afternoon the previously selected finger man of the group would call another member and announce, "It's your turn tonight."

That obligated the designee to furnish supper for the whole tribe, an expanding dozen hungry creatures, but not one cent could be spent. Whatever happened to be in the house was it. A typical menu might include a bushel of windfall peaches, dry bread and tea. One famous main dish was concocted from creamed onions and stale Ritz crackers. We never went hungry and we didn't dig into our bank accounts for entertainment either, because there was plenty of talent among us. Two year old Gail could perk up any proceedings. Born when her pretty white haired mother with the snappy dark eyes was already grandmother to a cluster of children, Gail seemed to have come equipped with the collective knowledge of her nephews and nieces. I clearly remember her announcing that she wanted to show us something and didn't need any help to get it. Carefully pulling out the drawers of a high-boy so that they made steps, Gail climbed to the top and opened a cupboard door. Disappointed that the object of her search was not there, Gail stamped a tiny foot and yelled, "God damn it, it's gone."

One of our group could tell startling tales of her clairvoyant experiences, and another knew a flock of good stories about the residents of the home for nice old ladies where Jane worked as recreation director. One of her pets was a ninety year old beauty whose oldest son was a very famous man. Whenever the son came to visit, the old dear would propel him around the home to introduce him proudly.

"This is my son Evan. He's my love child. Isn't it wonderful how you always love the most the one you had before you were married?"

Lee was the one with the best stories. One time when we assembled on the sand at Headlands Beach for a supper of onion sandwiches and pineapples, Lee began discussing the antics of the mythical Hoodwinkle family who at sometime in their long career had lived next door to each of us. As if we had rehearsed for a month, every Pauper contributed a chapter to the saga, and gradually an outer circle of strangers sat down to listen. The episode that broke up the picnic was how Lee had witnessed Mrs. Hoodwinkle taking off her petticoat to use as a milk strainer, at the same time that she spanked the youngest boy with the water dipper.

When Lee married and moved away, he ran out of time at the last, and my sister offered to clean his apartment for him. Lee was grateful, but probably sorry later because Marge found amid his junk a bunch of postcards Lee had bought while on a trip to France. Evidently he'd taken a few minutes to write flip messages, but had never addressed the cards, and that gave Marge an idea. With ink eradicator, she removed his signature, substituting such names as Hubert and Lyndon and Dickie and Zsa-Zsa and addressed them all to Lee himself. It would have been too easy to send them all from our town so she mailed them first in letters to Cucamonga and Wapakoneta and Castle Falls, and her correspondents sent them out. That trick did get a rise out of Lee when he finally figured out what had transpired, but we haven't heard from him since.

The rest of the Paupers are still the people I want most to see when I am in their area, and they are as interesting now as ever. Gail is eighteen now, as pretty and clever and delightful as she was all those years ago. The rest of us may not be quite as beautiful but we still have stories to tell.

When I last saw Elspeth she was still reeling from the black humor of the incredible situations that surrounded her mother's death. Her mother was clear minded and capable to the end, and she gave explicit instructions that she was to be cremated with the least fuss possible. In order to assure her mother that it would all be taken care of discreetly, Elspeth went to the city, fifty miles away, to make arrangements, coming back to tell her valiant mother that everything was under control. However, when the mother died and a call went out to the funeral director, he said he was awfully sorry but he'd lost his lease on the funeral home. He could still come, but the hearse had been stored out in the country in somebody's barn and it would take him a while.

Well, that was all right, Elspeth said, another hour wouldn't matter. The harried director called again some time later to explain that the hearse wouldn't start because the battery was dead, but he would be able to borrow a vehicle from a brother mortician. Eventually the trip was accomplished and instructions given that the ashes were to be kept until called for. Two weeks later Elspeth was considerably startled to have her doorbell ring and the mailman hand her a box clearly marked as from the crematorium, but that was not the end of the matter. In another few weeks there came a tearful, deeply apologetic call from the city.

"We don't know how to break this news to you, and we feel terrible about it, but we just can't find the box containing your mother's ashes anywhere." Elspeth says that her reply would not be printable.

Permanent friends like the Paupers go through many crises together, and I guess that requirement makes Earl one of the permanent ones. A Unitarian coffee hour is such a great place to meet people that many folks skip the sermons and show up only for the Java and jollity. Calvin was a fellow I met that way in Cleveland, although he wasn't a Unitarian, but just a man with a single great idea he was trying to sell. He wanted to establish in our society the mandatory practice of forever divorcing sex from reproduction. All that would be necessary, he preached, would be for every man to contribute to a national sperm bank and then be sterilized.

When children were desired, a couple who had been certified as fit to raise a family would trot over to the sperm bank and order a dose of sperm from good clean stock, high level sperm from which high level children could be conceived. Calvin never thought we were very funny when we tried to point out that all the babies of a certain period might then be sired by the same national hero, and we might end up with whole generations of Agnew or Namath kids.

But to get back to Earl. One reason I feel more comfortable in Unitarian churches is that they always attract a larger percentage of tall people, but Earl is outstanding even in Pierce Hall. Head and shoulders over all the rest, a girth to match, and skin the color of a smooth F sharp, I always knew when Earl was in the room. One of his first remarks to me was that I should get out my dancing dresses because we'd be stepping out a lot that winter. It was a promise he didn't get around to keeping, but he did come to cheer me when I was hospitalized, and I loved his midnight telephone calls that broke the tension engendered for him when he studied late into the night. Earl was a government economist at the time, trying to finish the thesis for his master's degree. After a few years, I suspected that Earl was really an eternal student, an activity that excused him from a lot of unnecessary socializing. I haven't really seen much of him over the years, but he did see me through one bad crisis in my life. It was at the time of my last great job hunt, when door after door was being slammed in my face because I was over-qualified or under-specialized or too old. Earl kept telling me to try the board of education, and I always resisted his advice. I said I wanted no part of the madness of the public schools, but finally the day came when my last hopeful application frittered away, and I called Earl in hysterics.

"Try the school board," he repeated. "I've been telling you that for six months, stupid."

That time I listened, and was shortly interviewed with simple, matter-of-fact courtesy. Certainly I could have a job. I was alive, wasn't I? I had the right credentials and presumably I was smart enough to find my way to the northeast side of town and report for work. I have blessed Earl ever since.

Earl never forgets to send me cards for birthdays and other occasions, and they get prettier all the time. Whenever I'm in Washington, he invites me to go to dinner. I don't expect him to follow through on these dates because I know he's too busy studying, but he did call me clear across the country and apologize the last time. The phone bill wouldn't worry him. Now that he is retired on three pension plans, he has more money than he ever had when he was working.

Years ago when we moved to Virginia, Connie and I were devoted to the pastime of exploring country roads, and one day we took along a neighbor on the assumption that since she was a native Virginian, she could lead us to all sorts of picturesque and exciting spots. As an adventure docent, Annie proved to be a wash-out. Way back in her insecure childhood she had shackled herself to a neurotic principle that she thought would protect her from life's mud-holes and vicious beasts. It read like this: Never drive down a road you haven't been on before.

It brought to mind the way nice parents impress on their children that they must not talk to strangers. My parents, being cut from a different roll of dry-goods, didn't hand down such ridiculous rules, but it wouldn't have been any use if they had. All the Crawford kids were born sensing that everyone was a stranger until you got to know him, and if you didn't get to know strangers, you'd have a pretty thin time of it.

Most of the people I've loved, tried and true friends, permanent and temporary ones, were once people I didn't know at all and was not introduced to. We didn't have debuts on Bloody Run, and I haven't attended many soirees since, but I have ridden on busses and planes, picked up hitch-hikers and thumbed a few rides myself, worked for a living, and washed my dirty clothes in numberless laundromats. That served the same purpose. I never cease to marvel at the way one thing leads to another, to use an old trite expression. To be a little fancier I could say that there is a silver thread of circumstance that leads to ever new relationships, all tied together like a maze. Certainly there are many dead ends in the maze, but some of the pathways lead to the foot of the rainbow, and some go right on over that brilliant bridge.

On the first leg of my nine month cross-country camping trip I stopped in central Virginia to visit a former student. His family had lived in the same house since before the Civil War, and Kirk was always trying to clear out some of the treasures that had accumulated; so he presented me with a stack of old National Geographics. He thought I might be able to hand them out to children along the way. As I was wandering through Montana later, I parked in the shade of a village square one hot afternoon and read the July seventy-one issue, and I was very much interested in the story about the Surprise Creek Hutterites. That day as the sun was beginning to sink, I saw the same sign advertizing fresh eggs that had guided the Geographic reporter, and took the same turn-off. Stopping beside a long skirted woman who was working in a flower bed, I asked about eggs. She was just as curious about me, a lone woman with a far away license plate, as I was about her, with the result that I stayed for the night and had the rare experience of knowing well these devout and friendly people who have chosen a simple, communal life. I had supper in the colony dining room, went pea picking with the women, and talked far into the night with my hosts and their children before settling down for a night's sleep in a hand made bed. The Hutterite colonies want to encourage communal spirit but they do not want to discourage family unity, and they know how much eating together as a family group can mean. No Hutterite house contains a kitchen, but each family has a hot plate and a trap door leading to a well stocked storage cellar. After we came home from pea picking, Mr. Walter said he was hungry and his wife should bring out the food. While we feasted on home-canned peaches, bread and cheese, and German chocolate cake which was that week's family treat supplied by the current cook, Mr. and Mrs. Walter asked me what life was like out in the world. When I told them about my former job in the school system, they assumed that meant I was a psychologist, and asked in great excitement if I had brought along any intelligence tests.

Although Hutterite children are not encouraged to be educated beyond elementary school and must leave the Colony if they insist on college, these parents, like most Americans, wondered how bright their two little children were in comparison with the rest of the country's scholars. Mrs. Walter asked if she could talk into my tape recorder so that I could take a message to her twin sister who lived in another colony in Canada, and in that way I went on to visit with other groups. Someday I hope to go back. They have given me a standing invitation to help them with the summer work, and I just might put on long skirts myself and take them up on the idea.

For a few months in 1972 I lived in one of my sister's little houses that she inherited from Uncle Walter.

Located in Bloomington, California, the house needed extensive repair and refurbishing before it could be rented or sold. Since I had neither stove nor refrigerator there, I took at least one good meal a day across the street in a little restaurant. I'm not sure whether the Hash family who ran it ever made any money, but they certainly had devoted customers, some of whom came for breakfast and stayed for supper. June would fill orders until her feet gave out and then she'd be likely to shake her head at the next request for ham and eggs.

"I'm tired, old buddy. You just run around the counter and help yourself to coffee. Have a doughnut if you're hungry, but you've probably had enough calories today anyway."

That was the kind of place it was. We all liked it and came to like each other. There was one steady customer who was unemployed while he waited, quite literally, for his ship to come in. We didn't have any body of water near Bloomington, but Bob had built himself a concrete ship. On his way to the coast, some sleepy trucker demolished the mammoth, and Bob couldn't begin another project until the lawsuit was settled. The insurance companies weren't sure how to proceed because they'd never had a shipwreck on the desert before. Bob was the man who set me on the path to Prescott, of which I had never heard before.

When the smog got so bad you couldn't see the car ahead on the freeway and my breathing suffered, I rented the house to another cafe customer and loaded up the camper. Just as I was about to take off in any direction I could escape the smog, Bob left his coffee cooling on the counter and came running over.

"Say, Ellen, I've been wanting to tell you to try Prescott, I liked it there and I think you would too."

I had never considered Arizona as a possible attraction. So far as I knew, it was all hot and dry, but now I zoomed across California like a road runner, found the town as enchanting as Bob had predicted, and I've lived here ever since. Prescott has a program of summer activities on the plaza, which is the local name for the courthouse square, and it was there at a dance one Friday night I met a genial old bear named Ed. Ed didn't think he was much of a dancer, and he announced from the start that he didn't want to get attached to anyone, but he did like to have a good time. Very shortly he annexed half a dozen of us unattached females to be his special pals. He took us out for hamburgers and fish fries, ice cream cones, and rides on the wild mountain roads. Sometimes it was one of us and sometimes the whole gang, but after each jaunt with only Myrtle or Alice or me, Ed would say, "Now let's go see Bobby, (or Betty, or Nora.)" After one long afternoon in which we had meandered along barely visible roads, the kind where you have to get out every few miles to open a gate and then drag it shut again, Ed and I had barbecued beef at some cross roads diner, and Ed suggested that we go see Myrtle.

That was how I found this wonderful little house in Myrtle's back yard where I have lived so happily. Myrtle is a white-curled blue eyed lady who never quite made five feet. She is always ready for fun, especially if it includes dancing. We have Mutt and Jeffed around town to swap meets and art shows, to dump picking forays and mountain camping, and we take in every possible dance. We have enjoyed building concrete steps down the ravine and cooking suppers together for all our friends, and we inspire each other to better organ and piano playing. Ed's harem is all broken up now, since most of the women aren't unattached any more. Ed is married too, to a woman who was out of town that summer, which was probably why he didn't want to get attached to any of us, but he did weld us all together in firm friendship, and he also proved in his kindly generous way that a summer romance is possible at any age, even for very proud widows like Myrtle.

Myrtle said from the beginning that she didn't care what I did to her cottage. Since I was determined to have a fireplace, she suggested that I knock out the front wall and enclose the little porch, and I have done that. One summer morning when I was out doors, coffee cup a-brim, admiring our handiwork, I realized that the old porch roof was in poor condition. Rapping on Myrtle's window, I asked her if she knew what day it was.

"Friday?" she guessed, all unsuspecting that it would be a day we would never forget.

I set her right. "This is the day you and I put on a new roof."

Myrtle is game for anything. "I was planning to sit around and read today, but you go get the roofing stuff and I'll be ready when you come back."

We had a beautiful time up on the roof under the blue Arizona sky, as we slammed in the roofing nails and covered ourselves as well as the roofing laps with sticky black goo. Several times I mistakenly threw off little pieces of roofing paper that Myrtle had carefully cut to fit in corners. When I offered to climb down and find them, Myrtle wouldn't let me.

"What makes you think I can't get my own scraps?" she demanded. "I'm only seventy-five, and I need the exercise."

I didn't do the rest of that remodelling myself. My young friends Tom and Cindy helped me with the hardest parts, and the way I met them is another story.

I'd been in California, and on the way home I was dumped out with a few other passengers at Wickenberg to wait for a connecting bus. I had climbed to the top rail of the fence and was exchanging pleasantries with a fair young man who said he was from Prescott too, when a mournful young woman with soulful eyes approached us.

"Do you know my sister in Prescott? I'm not sure where she lives but her name is Lizzie Logan. Oh, I'm so scared. The bus driver put me off here because I didn't have a ticket and I don't have any money and I'd be so afraid to stay outdoors all night."

"I could lend you the money to go to Prescott," the young man offered.

That wasn't quite what the little Nell had in mind. "Oh, no, I don't want to go there. Lizzie might not be home. I just wondered if you knew her."

"I'll give you a dime so you can put in a reverse charge call and find out if she's home," I suggested.

The girl threw me a baleful look. A dime indeed! "I'm really on my way to Los Angeles. Could you lend me the fare to go there and maybe for a few nights in a hotel until I find a job?"

She wasn't addressing me, but the man who became my good friend Tom. He said he didn't have that much money with him. Then she wheedled for ten dollars which would be more than ample to take her to Salome, the next little town west, where she thought she knew a fellow who was cooking in a restaurant. Just to be mean, I offered her the same dime to find out if her friend was really there, but time ran out and good kind Tom lent the artful beggar ten bucks which she promised to return real soon. Tom and I talked all the way home, and Tom explained that he believed there just might be some truth in the girl's plight.

Soon afterwards Tom invited me for chicken dinner, and when Cindy came to Prescott so that they could be married, he brought her over to meet me. I went to their wedding, drove them to Nogales the next year when they decided to have their first baby in Mexico, and welcomed them back to town with their little Joshua. Now that they have taken on the task of being house parents to ninety young women at the college, and have another son as well, we don't have as much time for afternoons in the pine woods or evenings by the fireplace, but they still help me with major projects. Tom and Cindy invited me recently to dinner and theater at the college. It was the kind of play in which the characters are out to prove that they can't survive five minutes without another drink, and the three of us agreed happily that we'd much rather be the kind who get our fun out of people.

I hope Tom and Cindy and their children are always nearby, but I'm well aware that one cannot order one's pleasure and comfort in this life.

Since many of my friends are worth a book apiece, I can't begin to tell here about all of them. I'm glad when friendships go on and on, but I can appreciate short deals too.

Over a glass of carrot juice in a health food store last fall I met a jolly seeming fellow who looked like a whaler captain dressed for a trip north. I knew he was a newcomer since residents don't put on fur caps and heavy mackinaws just because the thermometer registers twenty on a nice morning. We got to talking, and in the next week we went dancing and mountain hiking and howled with laughter over a game of phonetic scrabble. I think we reached the high point of our two week association when Bill brought over his guitar, and we went thru my song books to see what beautiful music we could make together. When we stopped for a bowl of soup, Bill fixed a clothespin on the page we'd reached and said we'd begin there the next time.

There never has been a next time, because Bill couldn't believe he'd found the greatest place on earth so easily, and decided to hit the trail again. It crossed my mind when he came to say good-bye that maybe I should have worked out that friendship meter anyway, but then I guess it wouldn't have helped much. I'll just keep the clothespin on Santa Lucia in case he decides to come back this way.

MOTHERHOOD AND FATHER FREUD

11

In the old days before the family had telephones, it was the custom for visiting relatives to bang on the door and yell "Surprise!" Travel being so uncertain, with mud roads, little money for gasoline, and every boy cousin over twelve fighting for his turn at the wheel, journeys were begun only for occasions like important birthday parties or ESP calls for help. Such was the time we had no food at all, and Aunt Mary responded to my mother's worry wave length by chugging in with the touring car loaded down with apples, potatoes and canned stuff.

In the opening remarks of my newborn Meredith, I thought I heard that old happy cry of "Surprise." Her trip to birth was fearsome too, accidentally commenced, and pursued despite the earnest advisors, including a part of myself, who chanted that it was criminal to bring a child into an unstable home in an unstable world.

One nicely brought up girl, who married into our family before she had a chance to meet all her husband's relatives, was asked when she planned to have children.

"Never!" the girl returned icily. "Aren't there enough Crawfords in the world already?"

Without being able to solidify the sentiment so neatly, I somehow shared her belief that it would be a dirty trick on unknowing protoplasm to shape it into even half a Crawford, but as babies sometimes do, Meredith tricked the birth control clinic, her resentful father and apprehensive mother. On top of all that, I got stuck with Dr. Cutter, a hostile obstetrician who never gave me a reassuring word but only grim attendance laced with sarcasm. Not at all pleased when I checked in to the hospital three weeks early, he sent me home again the next morning saying that it was a false alarm.

Unable to locate Elgin, and doubled over with nonlabor pains, I hastily caught the wrong street car, from which I was evicted onto the fifteen below zero steppes of the Western Avenue wasteland. It was my lucky day though, for I was able to reach home and do the washing before starting back to the hospital. No rooms were available. They put me behind a screen in the breezy hallway, where it was convenient for every passing intern to slip on a rubber glove and check my progress. They had a standard joshing summary with which to cheer a first time mamma.

"No one's ever travelled that road before, mother. It will take a long time."

After the tenth exam I was ready to chew the examiner, since supper trays went by and none for me, breakfast and lunch ditto. Nothing interrupted the parade of interns except the blazing pains, but then suddenly someone skidded my bed into the delivery room, just in time for Dr. Cutter to dump onto my stomach a chunky bundle smeared with what looked like cold bacon grease.

I heard his rasping voice in jovial camaraderie with the nurses. "When this one walked in, I was scared to death. But then I figured if I could handle her, I could do anything."

I had thought Dr. Cutter was furious at choosing obstetrics when another specialty might have let him fight a lovely war, but like so many other people, the dear boy was only afraid of big women. That didn't matter any more. When they brought my little surprise to me, all snuggled in flannelette, my baby spread tiny pink fingers across a smile of triumphant amusement. She was so delightful that I was able to survive the doctor's puzzling instructions that I have nothing but liquids for three days.

Somewhere in my voluminous reading I had picked up the idea that parents mold a child's behavior and personality, but we were no sooner home than the six day old Meredith started shaping me. Through stiffened lips she informed me that she would state the intervals at which I might feed her, schedule be damned. I quickly embraced the idea of demand feeding. Four years later Meredith was joined with her dramatic little sister Connie, and between them they have been upsetting my notions of what is proper, comfortable, and dependable ever since.

Connie peaceably devised her own schedule until she was five months old, and then she decided to teach me what a monster demand can be. Without precedent she demanded a meal at three in the morning. Startled but biddable, I warmed the golden Guernsey. The next night she wanted more than eight ounces and gradually increased the order until the awful time she insisted on a full quart. Connie had been born in the same unstable world, and in a different unsuitable home life, but Duane loved little babies. Nearly anything Connie did was fine, but he put his foot down on her idea of installing a pipe line to the dairy barn. She screamed wrathfully for a few nights and then subsided. We thought we had taught her something, but later I could see she was just retreating to plan her next campaign.

At nine months, she refused outright to be fed anything unless the food could be placed in her mouth by her own sticky fingers. Dainty enough with pieces of carrot and stringbean, her method of pasting handfuls of mashed potato all over her face, where it was more convenient to stoke her mouth, was revolting. We were beginning to invent cute apologies for her feral behavior, when she quit that scene and began eating with spoon and fork as skillfully as if she'd been born with the approved clutch.

My girls alternated periods of reasonableness, Meredith being quite easy to live with, after I signed the basic contract, until she was past two. I don't know what changed her into a demon unless it was my failure with the Christmas decorations. I'd been telling her of the beauties of Christmas, and knew I'd oversold the business when I couldn't find a string of lights in all war-time Chicago. Thinking that such a small child would be pleased with less glittering efforts, I arranged popcorn and cranberries, but Meredith took one look and swept me a glance of bitter scorn.

Her baby voice denounced me. "You said there would be lights."

Shortly afterwards she entered the Year of the Temper Tantrum. We were moving back to Ohio, and Meredith began her performance in the bus station, mopping up all the puddles of dirty melted snow with her thrashing snow-suited body. Pleased with her audience response, she began issuing invitations later: "I think I'll have a tantrum at the table tonight."

Most parents claim vivid recall of how they cured some noxious childish habit, ending their recitals with, "And from that time on—."

Not me. Most of my daughters' problems simply faded out, never the result of my efforts except for one shining hour. Meredith had decided that the other side of the street must be nicer, and would run across heedlessly regardless of what I said. So one day I tied her into her little rocking chair until she would promise to cooperate. She yelled her rage for nearly sixty minutes before agreeing to trade self restriction for immediate liberty, and she kept her promise. It was well she did, because Connie was soon ready to muddle my mothering methods.

Scorning second-hand parent training devices such as the tantrum, Connie became the patient sufferer of mysterious illnesses and a prolific bed soaker. Having studied the emotional problems of children, I was sure she was reacting to Duane's sternness and mood swings as she out-grew babyhood, but I wanted a person who sounded authoritative to explain this; so when Connie was seven, we took her to a psychologist. She related well during the study. Duane and I took days off to present ourselves for the verdict. Expecting that Duane might find criticism pretty devastating, I was feeling sorry for him when the psychologist spoke the fateful sentence.

"Connie is an unusually intelligent and sensitive child who believes she is a nuisance in your life."

For heaven's sake, he was looking at me!

I was too shocked to marshall my defenses except for a little silent rationalizing. I was the kid's mother, wasn't I? Her patient, loving, understanding mother. Kids take being hollered at sometimes, don't they? They know mothers don't really mean the unkind things they say and do, don't they? I remembered an incident when Connie was five, the time I backed the car into a ditch and had to endure Duane's furious tirade as he yanked it out with the tractor. That same morning I lashed out at the girls for their inefficient and time-wasting ways, and Connie kindly waited all day before asking brightly, "Are you still mad? We know you were really mad at yourself."

It took me a while yet, but when I could no longer escape the truth that I was hurting my children, I started psychotherapy.

If I hadn't met that phony fortune teller in the middle of Lake Erie during a frightful storm, I might have begun therapy some twenty years earlier and had a more successful life to write about. I was enroute to a church conference, and everyone else was seasick but the fortune teller and me.

"Let me read your hand," she coaxed in a Bavarian accent. "One look at those lines and I can tell you what kind of person you are."

There was nothing I wanted less, being too much aware of how much unpleasant character I was trying to hide.

"I don't have any money." I hoped that would stop her.

"Money!" she scoffed, snatching up my hand like a vacuum cleaner with a bread crumb.

All I remember now about what she read was that I didn't like it. When I demurred, she flipped my hand back to me and declared, "You have no imagination."

She couldn't have hurt me worse if she'd said I was doomed to the electric chair. I'd always believed that I was clumsy, crude, ignorant, unlovely, and fat, but I had so much imagination I hardly lived in the world. My creative brain was as lively as a red hot hopper full of pop corn, and my favorite teacher believed that someday I would be a writer, but now I'd been told the truth. The water was waist deep on the dock when we reached Lakeside and I would have preferred having it over my head, but somehow I had to go on living with my ailing self-concept. Certainly I never wanted to risk exposing myself to anyone who could see through the dense thicket I had cultivated around myself.

Years later in social work school, I received sixty minutes of weekly supervisory conference whether I liked it or not; the spot light was turned full blast on my motives and methods in relation to clients.

"Now what exactly did you say when Mrs. X came to the door?"

"Well, I just said something about being from the welfare, you know."

"I can't know unless you tell me. Give me your exact words, what you did when you said them, and what happened."

With no scientific orientation, nothing but twenty-three years of misconception and shame, I wobbled home and went to bed exhausted after each session. It must have helped a little, because I was encouraged to go on in social work, although I still shudder remembering some of the decisions I made for other people out of the stew of my own mixed up values. When you choose adoptive homes for other people's children, you have to remind yourself often that God's choice of parents for hapless babies isn't always so wise either.

Many agreements I made with other people couldn't have been more stupid. I can still see myself nodding pleasantly when my friend Sammy, who was driving my car up a snowy hill, asked devilishly, "How would you like to pass a car going eighty?"

I had a long ambulance ride afterwards in which to wonder why I was such a fool.

After Connie's evaluation, I scheduled my first therapy appointment, rehearsing a synopsis of all my childhood sex impulses. This was quite difficult, because Erv was already a friend. He was a sit-up or lie-down type of therapist, and I chose to sit.

"I'll begin with the time I was seven years old and a neighbor boy went out to the woods with me to hunt a lost goat, and he said that if I would—."

Five crimson minutes later Erv commented, "You seem to be forcing yourself to talk about sex."

I was utterly undone. "Isn't that what psychotherapy is all about? I can only afford to see you once or twice so I've got to get it all said."

He told me that it was more relevant to explore what I was feeling and doing in the present, and that he estimated a year would be more like what I needed.

His words were like a cool breeze under a maple tree when you've been pulling weeds in the hot corn patch.

His fees were so reasonable that I was able to finance a year or so with him, and further time with George, the therapist to whom Erv referred me because he thought I should work with a stranger. He said that I was prone to believe myself obvious to anyone who knew me, and didn't realize the need for personally discovered explanations. The profound sensitivity and warm manner of those two healers guided me to becoming less demanding and critical of my children, less afraid of my husband, more secure about life. If I didn't show progress in my secret wish to become slender, it was probably because I kept that agenda too secret.

Feeling so relieved and enlightened by my relationship with two such sapient leaders, for some time I believed in psychotherapy as if it were religion, until I met the wierdos in the field, like that guy who hissed to a frightened patient, "You are mentally ill and must be in hospital right now," thereby reducing her to the proper pulp for his panacea, shock treatments.

Neither do I like the Four Letter Men, so busy revelling in their inhibitory releases that they can't listen. They stop up their ears with toilet paper and embroider each sentence with copious references to defecation. Then there are the violators, or rip-snorters. For years a platoon of people-helpers tried to send a certain neurotic grandmother to a psychiatrist. She'd snatched the son of a daughter she had demoralized for years, and was working on him when we trapped her somehow into seeing a therapist. Dr. Marion bragged that he told her, "Why don't you take the kid out in the field and crucify him? You'll get it over faster that way."

There was the therapist who slept through his interviews, and the psychiatric group quack in Washington who loved a certain kind of problem. He always asked for audience contributions, but if the right situation was not forthcoming, he always had stooges more than willing to oblige. In one tawdry act a Thurberian female threw herself upon the startled visitor who'd shakily agreed to be a standin for her long dead father, and she poured out her well-rehearsed lusty wishes.

"Father dear," she moaned. "I happen to have a letter here that I wrote to you." Pulling out a wad of seven beat-up, closely written pages, she read us the whole damn rigmarole!

I suppose it did some good. Hardly anyone left with secret oedipal wishes.

I've known some of the truly great therapists, including Fritz Perls, considered by the Cleveland group with whom I studied to be the king. I saw him once settling down for a nap while a party in his honor went on without him. He said he was tired and expressed doubt that therapy was any use.

"I can strip anyone of his defenses in twenty minutes, but give him another twenty and he'll build them all back."

At a dramatic incident in a conference at Temple University, I heard another eminent therapist whose name I never learned because his thunderous speech was impromptu. The scheduled speaker had just told the following joke:

"An old experienced psychiatrist and a young one took the same elevator to go home one night, the older one spruce and debonair, the young one weary and tired. The novice asked the older man, 'How can you look so fresh after listening to people's troubles all day?'

"The older man smoothed his mustache and said, 'Who listens?' "

There was general laughter except from the intense man who strode to the platform and grabbed the microphone.

"Who listens?" he demanded. "By God! I do!"

The silence of outer space fell over the hall.

Having pored over the case histories of Freud and Reik, I was excited to have the opportunity to hear Theodor Reik at a seminar in Michigan. Vigorously enthusiastic about his work, he talked about his old teacher and his beliefs regarding the nature of man, commenting that a decadent society expected the children to emulate but not surpass their elders, while a progressive society encouraged the young to forge ahead.

I felt impelled to ask a question. "Dr. Reik, do you think that you have surpassed Dr. Freud?"

He spat out his answer. "Certainly not."

I was sorry I'd unmuzzled the old adolescent upstart in me.

Our family was certainly progressive, the way Meredith was attempting to reach the heights, indicating so tactfully how I could shape up to be more help to her.

"Mom, have you noticed how trim and neat Madalyn's mother stays? I picked up some pamphlets on good food habits I thought you might like to see."

"Bonnie's mother doesn't find it much trouble, she says, to fix up a nice buffet with salad molded in the shape of a fish, and everything served so nicely."

"I wish we could get this family better organized. When you go to Karen's house, you don't have to wonder how much junk will be on the dining room table. They have one beautiful vase of flowers on polished wood. I like that."

I felt sad and ashamed when it came through to me how much Meredith was suffering because she hadn't been asked to join a certain dancing class, but I had to have it explained why she wasn't going ahead making her own arrangements to join the fun.

"Go see about it, honey. Find out how much it costs and I'll try to find the money."

Her face crumpled in shocked despair. "You can't do it that way. Don't you understand? You have to be asked, and that's only if they think you're the right kind of people. They'd never ask me."

Refusing to believe that our town could be that snobbish, I made a few inquiries among some prestigious people I knew, and Meredith received the invitation, but I think the glow was a little dimmed for her to learn that the social majesties were approachable.

A few years later when Connie got the same bid, she didn't care much, never being inclined to follow big sister. No one should ever have children to build up self esteem. My ego was battered from Meredith's upward mobility, but I should have been happy, for Connie blasted all my props out from under me with her journey down the success ladder. The trend may have begun with her early recognition that teachers are not goddesses, but sometimes cranky and inept guides for the captive young. Each year the light in her eyes was a little dimmer when school was mentioned, possibly because she didn't bother trying hard and may have been assigned to less inspiring teachers who further contributed to her poor record. In Virginia where success depended partly upon acceptance of the Southern point of view on that adored conflict, the War Between the States, Connie hit rock bottom. There she also met college students such as Jimmy.

Jimmy was such a darling that the teachers always passed him on with the statement that if he'd only try, he could do excellent work. "And it might be hard to believe," he said, "but I've never read a book through in my whole life. Now I don't even know how. I got into college after they turned me down by saying I wanted to give my heart to Jesus."

She also looked hard at Orson, who was so busy preaching on Sundays in country churches that he had no time to study and admitted that he had to cheat on Religion 302.

Connie wasn't very verbal in those days, but her attitude said very plainly, "If that's what goes to college, why bother?"

Even more disturbing to me than her anti-education bias was the way she twisted my casework philosophy of respect for the individual, no matter how he looks, to choosing her companions almost solely from among the sneaky-faced who scuttle out of sight whenever they see an adult. Blocking out of her mind scholastic obligations, she skipped school with dreary rebels, but she did manage to graduate with the devoted help of a few intellectual black students who couldn't allow a militant white girl to fail.

Both my daughters levelled off. Connie spent three years among the runaways and drug addicts, the apathetic and suicidal at Dupont Circle, participating with her wit and growing knowledge in the fountain edge discussions, and eventually decided that college might have something to offer after all. She turned out to be an honor student recognized for her rare qualities. Meredith is so involved in trying to raise the country's education standards for all segments of the population, and build a living city church, that she wouldn't recognize a social ladder if it were sent to her for Christmas,—she'd probably use it as a balancing toy for black eyed Indian kids. Both girls can be charming and beautiful when they feel like it. Sometimes they are pretty repulsive too.

Often I wonder what it was I did that made them into such wonderful human entities. Was it the way I walloped Meredith when I got exasperated because she neglected piano practice? I guess not. She seldom plays any more. Was it the way I lambasted Connie for sneaking out with a boy at fourteen? Couldn't very well be that. She still has more healthy respect for her own plans and ideas than mine. I would never in the world have advised her bringing home a giant, expensive, hungry Doberman when she was still a hand-to-mouth student, but I guess she is a little like her grandfather in believing that good things come your way if you aren't too fussy about sensible details. I can see the animal is a most intelligent dog, possibly capable of bringing home her own bacon, if times get too hard.

I certainly didn't provide my children with a secure happy home life or with kind, understanding, supportive fathers. All I can think of is that perhaps some of my crazy, illusory dreams rubbed off on their impressionable souls, dreams about a better life in a better world, and they might not need to spend so much precious time being disillusioned, since I made no secret of how often I fell on my face.

Of all the thousands of people I've known, no one has given me more than my daughters. They have led me to friends who became dear to me, pushed me into going on with my exciting plans for new homes, new jobs, and my last wild idea, a year long camping trip. They've enlarged my viewpoint by offering my services to entertain Mississippi democrats and Paraguayan students, to make sandwiches for peacenicks and laughter for theater audiences. Connie thinks she might have failed somewhere since I never went on to get a doctor's degree in sociology.

Champions for some years of opposite values, my daughters detested each other, thereby upsetting another of their mother's notions, that sisters naturally love and help each other, but they are very good friends now. They agree that I will probably need to be let alone to work out my own destiny. I appreciate their fairness and try to give them the same leeway.

In this mad world where all of us might be choking on our own pollution in a few more years, I suppose it is criminal to have such hopes, but I can't stifle a few private wishes that my girls will get married and produce a child or two, not to emulate their mother but to go a little beyond the thresholds where I reached my limits.